THE PEELER'S NOTEBOOK

POLICING VICTORIAN DUBLIN:
MAD DOGS, DUELS AND DYNAMITE

BARRY KENNERK

MERCIER PRESS

MERCIER PRESS
Cork
www.mercierpress.ie

ISBN: 978 1 78117 709 9

A CIP record for this title is available from the British Library

Printed and bound in the EU.

Endpaper image courtesy of the National Library of Ireland.

To my students at Belvedere College – if history teaches us anything, it is that a successful life depends, not on medals or future glories but on a life well lived, with and for others, in the present.

CONTENTS

ACKNOWLEDGEMENTS

Writing a book is not a solo enterprise; it requires teamwork and compromise. I would therefore like to thank several people who helped to make this one possible; firstly, my wife and daughters for their support. Thanks also to Brian Donnelly of the National Archives of Ireland, to Chris Swift and Berni Metcalfe of the National Library of Ireland, and to the staff of the Garda Museum and Archives at Dublin Castle. Last, but not least, I am extremely grateful to Patrick O'Donoghue, Wendy Logue, Mary Feehan, Alice Coleman and the rest of the team at Mercier Press, and to Rishi Arora and his team at Westchester Publishing Services for their professionalism and courtesy.

INTRODUCTION

The term 'Peeler' has, in modern parlance, come to refer to a police officer. It was coined shortly after the formation of Robert Peel's metropolitan police forces in London in 1829 and Dublin in 1836. Peel, who was undersecretary of Ireland, planned to replace the old city watchmen, and the Peace Preservation force that followed, with a more organised corps of men. Regarding the title of this book, the term is more than simply eponymous. 'Peeler' recalls the well-known idiom about keeping one's eyes peeled; it suggests vigilance and alertness.

The Dublin Metropolitan Police (DMP) spanned an extra-ordinary era in Irish history during which unarmed constables encountered urban Ribbonmen, grave robbers and gun-toting Fenians. The history of the force, recounted by Jim Herlihy and others, is already well documented. What is less well known are the stories of ordinary policemen on the beat. Thousands of constables never had anything as dangerous or exciting as Fenian dynamiters to deal with, but that does not make their day-to-day experiences any less interesting. They walked miles in Dublin's fog-bound streets and encountered rabid dogs, visiting pickpocketing gangs from London, garrotters and ne'er-do-wells of all kinds. Their badge numbers were cited

Policemen were a familiar presence in Dublin courtrooms and they
were often asked to give evidence. (*The Graphic*, 22 January 1881)

in contemporary newspaper reports as they hauled thieves,
drunks and murderers to court and thus became an essential
part of the fabric of Dublin city.

For obvious reasons, policing was an extremely important
part of the British state apparatus in Ireland. The officers who
walked the beat with their Tudor crown and harp insignias
represented the authority of the state on a daily basis. The
DMP employed approximately 1,100 officers of all ranks.[1] By
the 1890s Irish cities such as Dublin and Belfast were the most
policed in the United Kingdom, far outstripping urban centres
like Birmingham, Manchester and Sheffield, each of which
had populations greater than Dublin. In fact, there was one
policeman for every 330 residents in Dublin, whereas the ratios

in Liverpool, Glasgow, Manchester and Birmingham varied from one in 480 to one in 580.[2] The primary reason for this high ratio of officers to people stemmed from the disturbed state of the country, and their role was evidently considered important enough for a provision to be included in the 1893 Home Rule Bill ensuring that the force would continue to be paid directly from the British Exchequer and remain answerable to the lord lieutenant.[3]

In some respects, the DMP appeared to be on an equal footing with its London-based counterpart, both in name and composition. The London Metropolitan Police was answerable to the Home Office rather than to the government, and likewise, the DMP reported to the chief secretary at Dublin Castle via the Office of the Police Commissioner. Part of the reason the forces had been set up like this was to offset any public fears about the development of a police state. Nevertheless, there were also key differences, for, unlike their British counterpart, the Irish police tended to be regarded as a colonial force. This was exemplified by the visit to Ireland by the colonial governor of Honduras in July 1893, who, having formally inspected the DMP and Royal Irish Constabulary (RIC) at a Dublin parade ground, told them: 'In the colonies with which I have had to do, we have made this force a model both as regards your organisation as well as the happy condition of things which has brought about its efficiency and utility.'[4]

However, that was not how officers of the DMP viewed themselves. Partly funded from the city rates, they did not see themselves as enforcers for the Crown. They tended to be more liberal in outlook than those who joined the semi-militarised RIC in the countryside, and the unmarried men who lived in local stations were, for the most part, free to discuss the events of the day such as Home Rule or Fenianism. This happened despite instructions laid down since the beginning of the force that a policeman was 'to abstain from the expression of any political or religious opinion, in any manner calculated to give offence'.[5] In truth, however, Robert Peel, who had become home secretary for the second time in 1828, had always been quite pragmatic on this point, telling the Irish chief secretary on 14 August 1829 that although 'all party distinctions in the police are forbidden ... the regulations in that respect cannot be too scrupulously enforced'.[6] That is not to say, of course, that caution was not needed. In 1843 a DMP sergeant was dismissed from the force after he attended a talk at the Rotunda to celebrate the Catholic gunpowder plot to blow up the Houses of Parliament in 1641.[7]

At times, ordinary constables were armed, but that was usually only a temporary measure in response to Fenian violence. Once the threat had passed, the weapons were returned to the headquarters of the various police divisions. Assistant Commissioner John Mallon, a very famous Dublin detective who became assistant commissioner in 1893, anticipated the words of the first commissioner of the Civic Guard, Michael Staines, several decades later, when he adopted the philosophy that his men should keep control through consensus rather than force. 'The only arms we carry are the baton,' he said, 'and the arms which nature has given us.'[8] That Mallon reached the position of assistant commissioner was a great achievement for an Irish Roman Catholic.

By the 1890s the DMP was beginning to use new techniques to fight crime, such as anthropometric identification, and around 1906 fingerprinting made its first appearance. Over time, understanding of the need to preserve crime scenes increased, and whereas members of the public could trample freely over the area where a murdered person lay during the early decades of the force, towards the end of the nineteenth century these areas were cordoned off. Other techniques, such as the procuring of handwriting samples by surreptitious means (e.g., by inviting prisoners to write letters to loved ones), would be considered extremely illiberal today. However, when John Morley was appointed as Ireland's chief secretary in 1892, he readily lent his approval to such methods, adding in a memorandum to the inspector general of the RIC that those who were disposed to political outrage did not deserve the right to be cautioned by the police:

> To require the police to give the caution in cases of crime before arrest would simply cripple the detective machinery and almost effectively prevent the procuring of evidence. The instinct of a detective on the commission of a crime prompts him to discreetly pump, without caution, everyone he thinks is in a position to give information, including suspected persons, and to alter this would be [the] equivalent of telling the fox that he is to be hunted the following day.[9]

The National Archives in Dublin holds many official reports of this nature, written on heavy blue paper and submitted by those who occupied the higher echelons at Dublin Castle: the various superintendents and the assistant and chief commissioners of the DMP, as well as the chief secretary, to name but a few. But for the most part, these administrators were not given to sensationalism or hyperbole and so there is very little detail about the ordinary officers whose intelligence-gathering helped the establishment keep an eye on Victorian Dublin. Research can be an occasionally serendipitous endeavour, however, and while I worked on other projects, I encountered references to fascinating, and heretofore under-researched, aspects of policing. These include the threat posed by rabid dogs, the punishment meted out to grave robbers and the difficulties of policing foggy and sometimes dangerous streets. Some edicts, such as those prohibiting the throwing of snowballs, seem almost ludicrous today, whereas others, like the occasional arming of the force, were made in response to wider political events.

Another problem when attempting to write a book of stories about Victorian policing in Dublin is that officers very rarely put anything in print, and in particular they were strictly forbidden from sending grievances to a newspaper.[10] Thus, the potential for first-hand accounts is even more limited. In one or two instances, there are occasional personal glimpses into the lives of the DMP, and those accounts are published in this book. Overall, *The Peeler's Notebook* comprises a treasury of real stories about the policemen who served Dublin city, and their careers can be evaluated, not just in miles walked and streets covered, but in the lives they changed, for better or worse.

1

WALKING THE BEAT

The solitary form of a tall police constable is silhouetted against the fading light on O'Connell Bridge. Theatregoers stream past him, laughing and talking eagerly; fruit sellers, set up at their standings to benefit from the passing trade, call out rhythmically; the regular, beating heart of the city is measured in apples and oranges, nuts and sweet pears. His eyes watch the crowd, vigilant for signs of trouble.

In *The Charwoman's Daughter*, James Stephens provides a very evocative pen portrait of how Dublin policemen went out on duty every evening during the heyday of the DMP:

> Every afternoon a troop of policemen marched in solemn and majestic single file from the College Green Police Station. At regular intervals, one by one, a policeman stepped sideways from the file, adjusted his belt, touched his moustache, looked up the street and down the street for stray criminals, and condescended to the duties of his beat.[1]

In the beginning the men were required to wear their uniform at all times, even during their leisure hours, but later this was relaxed a little and they could wear civilian dress to go to the theatre.[2] Other stipulations were more onerous, however.

Constables were supposed to seek permission from the police commissioners to marry. Also, since the force needed to be active at all hours of the day and night, their beat was divided into three shifts. In practice this meant that there always needed to be a certain number of men in each police station. However, even those who were not working were liable to be called upon, and for that reason they needed to live near their station houses. At times they even had to sleep in their clothes so that they could deal with an emergency quickly.[3]

There were seven police divisions in the Dublin metropolitan area, designated A to G. In 1901 the region was expanded to accommodate new suburbs such as Glasnevin, Drumcondra and Clontarf, and each morning, runners went out from Dublin Castle to deliver orders to each of the divisional headquarters.[4] The only departments that covered the whole of Dublin were the detective, or G, division and the mounted horse patrol.

Policemen were issued with badge numbers that matched their division, and when they were on duty, they were not supposed to walk at more than three miles an hour so that they could be of most help to members of the public. Strolling at this measured regulation pace, they covered about ten miles per day and got to know all the characters and buildings of note in their areas. Their beat book told them the correct order in which they should police the streets and the time allowed on each corner, as well as the locations of turncocks and fire engines. If a policeman had to leave his beat to take a prisoner to a nearby station, he was supposed to inform a colleague, who would then take his place.[5] In principle the men were not allowed to drink on duty (although they sometimes did so), and they were not supposed to engage in idle talk. On 1 June 1844 DMP constable John Moore reported a police sergeant in his official notebook for 'holding unnecessary conversation with a man named Dwyer … at Clarke's Bridge for 4 minutes'. As a result, the sergeant was demoted to the rank of first-class constable, which meant a salary reduction of five shillings per week.[6]

MURDER OF A LADY IN DUBLIN.

Strangers attracted a lot of notice in Dublin. When Harriett Neill, a wealthy landowner, was shot and killed by an agrarian gang at her home in Brighton Road, Rathgar, on 27 May 1872, the gunmen were quickly found and arrested. (*Illustrated Police News*, 8 June 1872)

Dublin was quite a small city and strangers were easy to spot.[7] With a population of just a quarter of a million people, visitors stood out, and if they acted suspiciously their movements were quickly relayed to the authorities at the Castle. In January 1898 the police of B division reported that 'two suspicious characters who were loitering at Foster Place inquired … the name of [that] building … what the equestrian statue in College Green represented; the high column in Sackville Street and what the needle-like column in the Phoenix Park was'.[8]

So many things came under the purview of policemen in Dublin – illegal gambling and cockfights, pickpocketing and petty thievery, dog licences, drunkenness and cases of furious driving. Constables were also supposed to do as much as they could while out on the beat to suppress begging. *The Irish Constable's Guide* (1895) urged them 'when on patrol or beat duty … [to] make special inquiries about vagrants who may have been begging in the locality'.[9] Some of the rules seem quite archaic by today's standards. For instance, the *Guide* urged fines for 'any person who shall fly any kite or play at any game, or make

A traffic constable at a busy city junction, 1886. (Courtesy of Alamy Stock Photo)

or use any slide upon ice or snow, on any public road or in any street of a town, to the danger of the passengers'.[10]

James Stephens wrote the following about a constable on traffic duty: 'He knows all the tram-drivers who go by, and his nicely graduated wink rewards the glances of the rubicund, jolly drivers of the hackneys and the decayed jehus with purple faces and dismal hopefulness who drive sepulchral cabs for some reason which has no acquaintance with profit; nor are the ladies and gentlemen who saunter past foreign to his encyclopaedic eye.'[11] There were no traffic lights, so a police presence at every busy street junction in the city was essential.

Jarveys were often appropriated by policemen, particularly in urgent cases when they needed to take people to hospital. They could also be commandeered by constables when they needed to get to the scene of a riot quickly.[12] The DMP was put in charge of the carriage office where horse-drawn taxis were licensed, and punishment was meted out to cabmen who did not pay their licences or who drove too fast. In 1899 the licence of a car driver named John Bergin of Boyne Street was revoked and he was sentenced to hard labour for 'cruelty to his children'. He had whipped his two sons 'in a manner likely to [cause] unnecessary suffering or injury' and when the case came to court the police magistrate said that he had treated his son John with a 'devilish savagery'. His licence had previously been revoked for assaulting a constable, drunkenness and furious driving, which had caused damage to property.[13]

In October 1839 a woman named Mary MacDonnell brought a complaint against a carman from Henrietta Place. En route to Kingstown (modern-day Dún Laoghaire), he insisted on stopping at a public house in Beggar's Bush for a glass of whiskey, which he drank. At Kingstown Church he became abusive and took the linchpin out of one of the wheels in his car, which rendered it immobile. However, when Mrs MacDonnell, who was a friend of the undersecretary, Thomas Drummond, called in to the local police station, she got no help. She later made an official statement which makes for amusing reading:

> The policeman told her to tell Mr Drummond to 'kiss his arse' and she might do the same … The same policeman shoved informant into the street and informant is now unable to proceed on her journey from the treatment she received, especially from the carman.[14]

There was a serious postscript to this incident. Magistrate Lynam ordered the head constable at Kingstown to 'parade' all of his constables at his quarters 'in order to ascertain the individual who conducted himself so'.[15] The authorities did not tolerate bad manners or discourtesy.

One of the more colourful arrests made by the DMP took place one Sunday in April 1859 when the entire detective division descended on No. 7 Essex Street to break up a cockfighting tournament. The cocks were put into a ring, booted and spurred, and wagers were put down by the various 'fanciers'. For months, the house had been a source of annoyance to local residents, but the owner had taken great care to let nobody in who had not been introduced or did not hold a shilling ticket.

Prior to the tournament, the police suddenly became 'most devout' and went to twelve o'clock mass at the nearby church of St Michael and St John:

> When mass had terminated, the gimlets who were in coloured clothes came out of the church in the midst of the congregation and, making a short turn, presented themselves in front of the Olympic circus. Before any alarm could be given, Superintendent Ryan and his men had gained admission and, in a few minutes, stood in the centre of the lists, where 37 individuals and Mr Ruth were enjoying a hard-fought rubber of 5s 10d. Nothing could exceed the consternation of the proprietor and the devoted 37 and, finding themselves trapped, various attempts were made at a cut and run, but escape was hopeless and they had to submit.[16]

The way in which policemen walked the beat reflected Victorian sensibilities. Only experienced officers walked the main thoroughfares such as Sackville Street, Dame Street or Grafton Street because they were considered knowledgeable enough to assist members of the 'quality' if they needed assistance, whether it was help in the event of a crime or directions to landmarks of interest. That left the new recruits or 'Johnny Raws' to patrol the dangerous laneways and backstreets of the city.

The area around Hardwicke Street was particularly notorious. At the rear of the nearby Temple Street Children's Hospital, founded in 1879, there was a piggery, a forge and horse stables interspersed with overcrowded tenement houses, and during the 1890s residents of Gardiner Row, Gardiner

Street and Temple Street (including the doctors of the hospital) signed a petition that they then sent to the chief commissioner of the DMP, informing him about the behaviour of the local inhabitants:

> The screaming, fighting and drunken brawls which are going on in it every night are an intolerable annoyance to the persons residing in the surrounding streets. We, the inhabitants of the above-mentioned streets, are unable to open our back windows on account of the filthy and blasphemous language which would then become audible, and pollute the ears of our wives and families. This annoyance is worse on Saturday when the drunken inhabitants of the Court are allowed to issue from it to the adjacent Streets, and disturb the neighbourhood until a very late hour without interference from the Police.[17]

The petitioners sought protection from the DMP and wanted them to make arrests. Failing that, they asked that enough officers be put on duty to deal with disturbances. It was understandable why a young officer, armed with just a few months' experience and a truncheon, might feel daunted going into such areas alone.

Unlike their semi-militarised counterparts in the RIC, the DMP did not give guns to their officers 'because of the rarity of homicides and serious personal violence in Dublin compared to the countryside'.[18] In response to the Fenian threat of the late 1860s, a ten-ounce truncheon appeared on the streets, but such weapons were useless against more sophisticated weaponry. The first police officer to be fatally shot on duty was Charles

O'Neill in 1866. When an armed detective named Clarke went in search of the killer, he was almost shot as he stopped a man for questioning in the damp quarters of a tenement hallway. Fortunately he was too quick for the would-be assailant and, seizing the gun, told him that 'he would send the contents thro' him if he attempted to resist'.[19]

In spite of the city coroner's recommendations, made in May 1866 and November 1867, that the police force needed to be armed, this was difficult to implement on ideological and practical grounds, and in August 1868 Conservative MP for Armagh Mr John Vance cautioned that:

> However well justified a policeman may consider himself in firing, the act with all its accompanying circumstances, whether the result be attended by loss of life or otherwise, must become the subject of legal investigation. It therefore behoves those who may be placed in such a situation to be well prepared to prove that they acted with becoming humanity, caution and prudence and that they were compelled by necessity alone to have recourse to their arms.[20]

Several policemen were shot in 1866 and 1867, and for a short time after each incident, constables going on the beat were equipped with firearms and sent out in pairs. However, this was quite a short-lived measure, and the weapons, mostly seized from Fenian suspects, were outmoded and often unreliable.

One of the biggest hazards faced by policemen on the beat was the city's myriad narrow lanes and alleys. For instance, the area behind Aungier Street, stretching as far as St Stephen's

Green, was a veritable warren of backstreets in which a red-light district of twenty-five brothels did a roaring trade, alongside six unlicensed public houses. In 'Monto', another red-light district on the northside of the city just off Great Britain (now Parnell) Street, underground passages led from the pubs into the brothels so the clientele could pass between the two undisturbed, and police raids brought constables into many dark corners, including the holds of ships on the River Liffey and opium dens.[21]

Their searches led them over walls into pig yards, down blind alleys and across stables, and they never really knew what they might come across. In August 1840 two policemen were beaten up by a retired army captain who galloped through Marlborough Street during the early hours crying 'fire, fire!'[22] On 28 July 1842 a destitute and starving woman broke a gas lamp on Thomas Street just so she could be arrested.[23] In August 1855 a twelve-year-old girl was discovered by police chained to an iron bar by her waist in a coal hole on Capel Street. She had been shackled so long by her father that she was unable to walk.[24] There was seemingly no end to the things a constable might see while on the beat.

The police may have lost sight of and rejoined their quarry under the shadow of high Georgian houses that backed onto small cottages, or across the cracked stones of moss-covered, time-worn courtyards. My wife's grandfather, Dick Fitzgerald, lived in Bow Bridge near Cromwell's Quarters in Kilmainham. Dick recalled that on one occasion he crept into a nearby yard with a young 'accomplice' to steal eggs from some chickens. With the first part of their mission accomplished, they sat on the landing, from which they had a good view of two policemen standing on a nearby street corner.[25] The local children nicknamed these two stalwart officers 'Thunder' and 'Lightning'. Thunder was a portly sort, but Lightning could run for Ireland. The two lads dropped the eggs on their heads. Dick remembered that Lightning chased him through the streets for two hours.

Seamus Marken, who lived near Moore Street market, recalls another legendary chase:

At that time, there was a big derelict tenement house in Little Denmark Street. There may even have been two, for that matter. People had pulled up the floorboards for firewood. At the back of it, there was a huge waste ground called the Ouler where there had been buildings of some kind, but in my day it was all flattened. We used to go and dig holes, make trenches and play war in it. When we'd be chased by the police for playing football or for jeering a copper, we'd have to run like hell through these markets. Once we'd get across the Ouler, we'd go through the tenement. You had to sort of hug the wall with the other foot on the joist. Then we were out into Denmark Street, Chapel Lane, Parnell Street and away.

Most policemen might chase you as far as the Ouler, but they wouldn't bother going further than that. One time, one policeman thought he was good, so he kept on chasing us. Of course, we ran through the building. He ran after us but fell on the joists. He started screaming. We had to get a man in Denmark Street to go in and get an ambulance to take him away. He could have been destroyed.[26]

Once a policeman had made an arrest, he needed to escort his prisoner to a local police station, but that was not always so easily done. Attacks on prisoner escorts were commonplace, and stone-throwing mobs often fell upon the constabulary, sometimes in gangs of 300 or more. Sticks and stones were used and, on extreme occasions, bricks, kettles, old basins and other objects were flung out of tenement windows.[27] Not all prisoners were unhappy to be arrested, however. Destitute people could look forward to a meal while they were in custody, as well as a roof over their heads.

In 1846 a Wicklow man named Lacy was arrested at a shop in Bride Street when he handed over a filthy crown-piece from the time of King George III. Because the coin was so old and worn, the shopkeeper accused him of counterfeiting. Lacy called for help from a passing constable, who took a dim view of the transaction and escorted him to Chancery Lane Station. Afterwards, a local silversmith was able to prove that the coin was in fact genuine, but the biggest surprise came when Lacy was freed and his wife arrived to meet him. She was delighted he had been locked up because that Saturday night an armed gang of agrarian activists, or 'Ribbonmen', had arrived at his home to kill him. Had he not been mistakenly arrested, he might have died at their hands.[28]

The station house to which Lacy was taken was a large and elaborate complex that featured a parade ground, coal cellars and office. In 1862 it was joined to the newly built Clarke's Court police barracks. Other station houses had been modernised prior to the establishment of the DMP. In 1828, for instance, an architect, assigned to make improvements to College Street Station, noted that it was 'rather in a precarious state' because the adjoining houses had been demolished, and he added that there was 'want of a room for transacting the public business'.[29] By the 1840s, however, many of the stations had cells for prisoners with ventilation in the roof and sufficient accommodation for the men, including a mess hall and kitchen. Responsibility for keeping them clean usually fell to an old charwoman who was sufficiently aged that she could not corrupt the morals of the constables.

By the 1880s telephonic communication had been established between the various police stations, as well as with the chief secretary's office at Dublin Castle.[30] Other innovations followed, such as the purchase of typewriting machines in 1889.[31] Such technology helped the police authorities keep pace with a growing population and, as the city expanded beyond the confines of the Royal and Grand canals, deploy men where they were needed most. For instance, the telephone was crucially important during the Burgh Quay disaster of 1905, and again in September 1913, when the Castle needed accurate information about the movements of rioters. However, these changes complemented, rather than replaced, good, old-fashioned police work and when an officer was faced with a dangerous or unusual situation, the most important tools at his disposal were courage, intelligence and a good sense of humour.

2

THE DUBLIN CHARLEYS

A flickering lantern casts an arc of yellow light, illuminating the warped glass panes and fanlights of houses that have seen better days. It falls onto the careworn face of an old city watchman, dressed in a greatcoat and three-cornered hat. He treads wearily over the dung-caked cobbles of a dark Dublin street. Between quaint gable-fronted Dutch Billy houses whose timbers creak and groan, he cries out the weather and the hour. 'Past eleven and a calm night!'

When the Dublin Police with its suburban Peace Preservation Force (Peace Officers) came into existence during the 1820s, followed by the DMP in 1836, it replaced the old eighteenth-century city watch. The watch comprised about twelve watchmen in each of Dublin's twenty-one parishes (a total of about 400) and was funded from local taxes. Each watch was put under the charge of a parish constable. The lord mayor (or, in the case of the Liberties, the seneschal of the manor) was supposed to inspect the men twice a year, at the beginning of May and November, and dismiss any who '[should] appear unfit for service'. Many of the men were old and infirm, however, and for the most part, they were very ineffective.

The watchmen were dressed in long frieze coats and low-crowned hats, and along with their pike staffs, they carried rattles which, when spun, made a very loud, harsh sound. Just like a policeman's whistle, this was to summon help in a dangerous situation. The city watch officers carried pike staffs and they could be fined if these weapons were mislaid or stolen. Written regulations dictated how the men were to patrol the city. For instance, according to a dictate of 1730, the watchmen were supposed to go out each evening from the watch house at Young's Castle, Oxmantown, then round a swampy area called the Little Green and finally to 'Bradogue Bridge', which was around the present-day market area behind Dublin's Four Courts.[1] They also served the area around Sackville (now O'Connell) Street. A minute book for 1750–70 describes the way in which they worked the beat at the southern end of Sackville Mall: 'To patrol to Mrs Lassey's in Henry Street back to Off [Moore] Lane, from thence to Doctor Robinson's round the Mall to his Stand.'[2] One of their main duties was to cry out the hour and weather: 'Past two o'clock and a storm is coming!'

In practice, however, the city watchmen often did very little real patrolling. William Richard Le Fanu, brother of the renowned novelist Joseph Sheridan Le Fanu, remembered them fondly from his student days during the early nineteenth century, and he described them as 'generally old and often feeble'.[3] During their youth, many of the watchmen had been

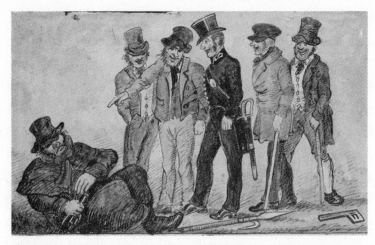

Drunken watchman lying on the ground with his rattle nearby, by
William Sadler, *c.* 1820.
(Courtesy of the National Library of Ireland)

domestic servants or held posts in Dublin Corporation, and during an era prior to the old-age pension, the city watch was an opportunity for them to avoid sinking into complete indigence.

The ineffectiveness of the watch allowed gangs of dangerous, wealthy, young men to roam the streets and terrorise people. These included the 'Mohawks' and the 'Cherokees'. One of the most infamous gangs was the 'Pinkindindies', so called because they cut off the ends of their sword scabbards, exposing enough of the blades to painfully prick unsuspecting victims without causing death.[4] The watchmen were unable to keep control with these groups running rampant.

In December 1775 a watchman was warned by two duellists on the streets of Dublin not to 'stir' from his box on pain of 'instant death' if he interfered.[5] In October 1790 another watchman was rushed by a mob of men dressed as Irish Volunteer militia, who rescued a prisoner in his custody and stabbed him, inflicting serious wounds.[6]

In June 1780 some gang members were able to 'seize' a young lady near Queen Street Bridge (Mellows Bridge) and carry her off in a horse-drawn chaise until her cries brought help and the vehicle fortunately overturned.[7]

In November 1778 a gang of Pinkindindies attacked the watch of St Andrew's Parish in Dame Street and 'cut and hacked some of them very inhumanly', and even though the watch managed to arrest the men, the prisoners were later rescued from the watch house by their friends.[8]

It was, of course, impossible for the watchmen to adequately patrol vast sections of the old city, and their wages were sometimes sporadic. During the latter half of 1808, the men were not regularly paid, and in September James Whiteside and Simon Hatch, clerks in the head office of police, were ordered by the police magistrates 'to pay the Watch Constables and Watchmen seventeen weeks, to 31 December 1808 inclusive'.[9]

There were, during the late eighteenth century, 450 streets, lanes, alleys, courts, rows, yards, markets and bridges, and there were only just over 300 watchmen on duty in that whole area. There are many recorded instances of crimes committed at times when the watchman's shelter or 'box' was empty. Indeed, it was said that 'a robber of genius can, by drinking a pot of ale with a watchman, know exactly at what time a post will be clear for the purpose of robbing securely'.[10] In April 1785 a young man had his money stolen in Anglesea Street, but the watchman did not arrive on the scene until after the thieves had escaped. When the victim told him that he had seen the robbers 'make into a particular place', the watchman 'insisted to the contrary' and took him in the opposite direction.[11] That is not to say that no arrests were made; following a successful apprehension for robbery, one watchman proudly wrote: 'I searched the prisoner and found the watch in the arse of his pants.'[12]

For the most part, the watchmen spent quite a lot of time smoking pipes and sleeping in their boxes, but the conditions were not all that pleasant and, inevitably, many of them suffered from rheumatism and chest complaints. They were given an allowance of coal so that they could fuel their braziers during cold winter nights, and in an era prior to gas lighting, they had candles to see by. Nevertheless, it must have been extremely cold at times, and an official government return for 1810 lists the provision of 'jackets and cloaks'.[13] Students from Trinity College used to creep up and steal their rattles or pike staffs, which they then displayed in their dorm rooms, not dissimilar to today's student trophies such as traffic cones and road signs. The biggest prize of all was to find a 'Charley' sleeping on duty and tumble his box over – face first, of course – so that when he suddenly woke, he found he couldn't get out. Inside the face-down box, his rattle couldn't be heard and he was bound to lie like that for a long time before he was rescued.

Nineteenth-century newspapers abound with incidents of 'knocker wrenching', which was a common occurrence in

Dublin, but this was merely one of the more harmless crimes alongside murder, serious theft and assault. One anonymous writer recalls how he and a roving gang of lads 'took off every knocker' around Merrion Square and then, not content with that, 'broke the lamps, and uprooted every bell besides'. They plunged the streets into darkness without fear of being stopped by the city watchmen, who 'scarcely had the strength enough to spring their rattles, and even when they did, they kept at gun-shot distance'.[14] Fortunately, they met their match when they reached the home of General Meyrick, a British soldier who had played a prominent part in suppressing the 1798 Rebellion in County Meath. He levelled a gun at them, which gave the timid watchmen courage, and they quickly moved in to seize the gang. The youths were sent to a local watch house to spend the night, but they were easily able to scale the wall and make their escape. When Robert Peel was chief secretary of Ireland in 1818, it was incidents such as this that prompted his interest in reforming the police service. Later, as home secretary, he went on to establish the London Metropolitan Police in 1829.

For a short time during the 1820s, Dublin city had a town police force with a suburban peace officer corps assigned to patrol the semi-rural hinterland, some of whom were mounted. This was a step in the right direction, but further change was required.

Thomas Drummond was appointed undersecretary at Dublin Castle in 1835. He was keen to introduce reform of the police service in Ireland, and the following year the parliament passed an Act for Improving the Police in the District of

Dublin Metropolis.[15] On 1 January 1838 the new DMP were proudly paraded in front of the Lord Lieutenant at the gardens of Dublin Castle for the first time, dressed in their frock coats and top hats.

The earliest entries in the DMP register show that some members of the old watch were recruited to the new force. The youth of many of the men is also noteworthy, putting paid to the idea that they were all old and doddery.[16] For instance, they included twenty-eight-year-old Patrick Kavanagh from Arklow, County Wicklow, whose name appears as the third entry in the book. Against his name, 'Old Watch' is recorded. Others were from Dublin, including Peter Cope, a twenty-six-year-old former servant. The new DMP also attracted a significant number of officers from the London Metropolitan Police; most were Irish, and some, such as Cork-born John Fitzpatrick, stayed with the force for many years, until retirement.[17]

3

THE NIGHT OF
THE BIG WIND

Shards of glass slice the air like broken stars; the shattered dreams of home and hearth stolen by the Banshee gale; the ringing of bells and the rattling of slates crashing to the pavement on Sackville Street adds to the awful confusion. A house facing the Bethesda Chapel at the corner of Dorset Street and Granby Row comes down with a horrible crash, filling the street with smashed planks, bricks and dust. The air grows hot with the flames of burning buildings.

The Night of the Big Wind, as it was later known, was (and remains) the most devastating winter storm to hit the island of Ireland in the past 500 years. The Sunday night when it struck in January 1839 was the Feast of the Epiphany, a time when, according to Irish folklore, Judgement Day would come and souls would have to account for their sins. It was cold, and most of the country was covered by a light dusting of snow. As the day went on, however, the temperature rose inexplicably, and some people felt a sense of foreboding, as if something were about to happen.[1] Overhead, grey, ominous clouds swirled slowly. Then,

THE SCENE AT Nº9 DORMITORY

Policemen helped to put out fires for most of the Victorian period. They needed to know where fire engines were kept and the locations of turncocks for water. (*Illustrated Police News*, 11 January 1890)

on Sunday evening, a breeze started to blow, jostling boats at anchor and stirring rubbish into little whirling dervishes on the streets. From that point on the wind worsened, and by the early hours of the morning it had reached the intensity of a hurricane.

The River Liffey swelled and burst its banks along the quays, and the wind, which roared like a freight train, was now loud enough to drown out any attempts people made to speak to each other. They could do little but take refuge indoors. They were terrified by the awful roar, and it seemed as though they were under attack from some malevolent, supernatural entity. All over Dublin, slates were ripped off roofs, and a stationer's house at the corner of Merrion Row and Baggot Row lost a stack of chimneys when they toppled and fell into one of the bedrooms, fortunately not killing anyone as the family had not yet gone to bed.[2] In nearby Cork Street, a woman was buried under a mass of falling masonry, and as far as twelve miles inland from the coast, trees were covered with salt brine.[3] Stones weighing up to 'two hundred weight' were hurled as if by the hands of giants off St Peter's Church in Phibsborough, and at the Viceregal Lodge in the Phoenix Park, a guard was lifted up in the air and carried across the park, fortunately sustaining nothing more than a broken arm. At the Guinness factory, nine dray horses were killed and a number of stables were flattened.[4]

Needless to say, the storm was extremely challenging for the fledging DMP, particularly as a city fire brigade had not yet been established. This meant that officers were pressed into service to deal with fires and to help free people from the rubble of houses. Some members of the force were on duty when the storm struck and took shelter as best they could. In Glasnevin a portion of the wall at the Botanic Gardens fell and crushed a policeman to death.[5] Within a short space of time people began to crowd into DMP stations as the full scale of the humanitarian disaster began to take hold. In the Liberties people whose little cottages had been badly damaged went from house to house seeking shelter, until eventually the local police station at Newmarket was overrun.[6]

At No. 40 Dawson Street, a party of constables worked hard to dig two servants from the rubble after the building collapsed; when they finally reached the pair, the constables were much gratified to find that they were still alive.[7]

During the height of the storm, at about two o'clock in the morning, a female inmate started a fire in the laundry room of the Bethesda Penitentiary and it quickly spread to the adjoining chapel. Messengers were sent to several police barracks in that area, but going out onto the streets was not without its dangers. Earlier that night, one young man who was turning into Sackville Street from Great Britain (Parnell) Street had been blown off his feet and dashed against a lamp post, fracturing his leg. Fortunately the same fate did not befall the Bethesda messengers, and within a short space of time a strong force of police had arrived at the chapel under the command of a Superintendent Rice and Messrs Murphy and Prendeville, inspectors of C division. Both inspectors were scorched on the head when they got too close to the burning buildings, and a private from the military was badly injured and later died.[8]

On their arrival, the police began working to put out the flames. Some constables were sent to the city corporation to get more help, as well as to the different insurance offices, which employed their own private firefighting services during that era. At five o'clock that morning detachments of military arrived, but the storm continued unabated and, despite their best efforts, the adjoining houses caught fire. It soon spread from Dorset Street into Granby Row, and the people living there began to take their furniture away to save it.

By now, fire tenders from several insurance companies were also on the scene: Atlas, West of England, Royal Exchange and National Insurance Company. Their hoses were rolled out and water was brought to bear on the blaze. However, as officers worked hard to bring the Bethesda fire under control, looters took advantage of the confusion to steal from some of the unoccupied houses.[9] When a constable attempted to haul one of the looters away to his station, he was attacked by a man named Joseph Flynn, as well as by a military corporal and a private, who tried to free the prisoner. Flynn grabbed the constable by the neck from behind, put a knee into his back and brought him to the ground. The constable was then kicked savagely by the three men and the prisoner. Meanwhile, one of the mounted constables was also attacked and his horse was kicked.[10]

The next morning, Dublin bore all the appearance of a sacked city razed to the ground by an invading army. Sackville Street was a scene of utter devastation, with slates off all the roofs, and on nearby Rutland Square stacks of chimneys had been blown in. Trees were either blown down or, in the case of those on the Royal Canal, torn up by the roots and thrown to the far bank. Several people were committed for trial before the magistrates of Henry Street division. This included five women and a soldier of the 7th Fusiliers, arrested for stealing £30 worth of jewellery from a home on Granby Row.[11]

In the aftermath of the storm, a quarter of the city's homes had been destroyed. Many people were left without a roof over their heads and some died afterwards from exposure or illness. As a testament to the impact that the hurricane had on the lives of Irish people, when the Old-Age Pensions Act was introduced over seventy years later in 1908, older people who didn't know their age were asked whether they could remember the Night of the Big Wind. For the DMP, the storm was one of the first times that the force came together *en masse* to help the people of Dublin. The events of 6 January 1839 tested the officers severely, but it also showed them what they were capable of when they worked together, qualities that would prove important over two decades later, when Fenianism was at its height, and during the 1916 Rising.

4

STRANGE CRIMES AND UNUSUAL PUNISHMENTS

There is a scuffle on St Stephen's Green as a well-dressed man, his hands trying frantically to grasp the cord choking his neck, is dragged backwards into a laneway by an unseen assailant. His sword cane, now lying useless on the pavement where he dropped it, might have helped him if he had had the chance to unleash the blade. Now, he is at the mercy of the garrotters, all for a few pound notes and a pocket watch.

During the early years of the Dublin police force, many of the rules and regulations that constables were obliged to enforce were quite strict; some might even be considered unusual by today's standards. A person could be fined for throwing snowballs, and prisoners were sometimes caned in police stations as a punishment.

One of the largest snowball fights ever recorded in Dublin took place during the winter of 1872–73. In February there was a good fall of snow, which gave the students of Trinity College an opportunity to come out in their hundreds and have a 'set to' with snowballs.[1] Shortly after eleven o'clock that morning, they formed themselves into attacking and defending parties, and the old buildings resonated with the cheers of the victorious as they drove their defeated friends from square to square. A torrent of snowballs hit the doors of the Examination Hall, disturbing the Court of Appeal proceedings being held there. Passers-by on College Green could hear the ringing cheers throughout the campus, and eventually the students made their way to Lincoln Place, where, in a force of 500 or more, they began to pelt some of the local coal porters.[2]

When the tenement dwellers returned with reinforcements, the fight got so heated that some of the local shopkeepers were forced to put up their shutters. The police tried to make some arrests among the students, but in the melee constables 45B and 158B were knocked down and kicked, and a Sergeant Nolan, who tried to help them, was cut on the head. One constable, who went too near the college railings, was taken prisoner by the Trinity students, who closed the gate and ran away with him through the campus. The other policemen then stormed the gate until it gave way, only to find that their captured comrade had been carried, unharmed, all the way through the college grounds and put out at the College Street gate.

Of course, some of the crimes the police had to contend with were more gruesome than mere snowballing. In May 1872 an English gang wreaked havoc in Dublin with a spree of gar-rotting attacks. The garrotte was a piece of cord used to stran-gle victims from behind. Indeed, this was not the first time a gang from Britain had come to Dublin to commit crime. On 22 June 1868 Superintendent Ryan of the DMP reported that some of his detectives had captured five members of the London 'swell mob' and that six more of the gang had returned to England.[3] The swell mob were expert pickpockets and house burglars. They were usually very well dressed and frequented racing events and other places members of the gentry were known to attend.[4] When they were arrested, they did not usually put up much resistance.

ALLEGED GARROTTING AND ROBBERY

There was a spate of garrotting attacks in Dublin during the 1870s. (*Illustrated Police News*, 12 November 1870)

The garrotting gang that came after them was far more dangerous. Within the space of about a fortnight, they strangled twelve people, several of whom they also robbed.[5] One intended victim was a gentleman named Alexander Thorp of North Cumberland Street. On 21 May 1872 he was attacked on Ranelagh Road while out walking with two ladies. A man came up behind him and attempted to catch him by the throat. When Thorp drew back, his assailant whistled for help and a second man emerged from the shadows. Thorp then drew a

CAUGHT AFTER A CHASE OF HALF A MILE.

Garrotte attacks continued into the early years of the twentieth century. (*Illustrated Police News*, 1 December 1906)

dagger from his breast pocket and, according to *The Freeman's Journal*, cried: 'If either of you come a step nearer to me I will plunge this dagger into you. I know who you are and what is your purpose.'[6] This was enough to warn the attackers off and they fled the scene.

There were several ways that members of the public could protect themselves from such criminals. Just a few years earlier, at a meeting of the Anti-Garrotte Association in London, its secretary revealed that an anti-garrotte device, a steel collar with spikes in it, had saved him seven times. As a result, sales of the device soared. At the same meeting, a second device was described – a pair of gloves, each one of which had two curved steel hooks in it, about the size and shape of a parrot's claw, on the middle finger and thumb.[7] These were designed to slash at and wound an attacker. On 20 December 1862 *Punch* magazine published the 'Song of the Anti-Garotter', and one of the verses ran thus:

All around my neck, I wear a spiked steel collar,
A revolver and a bowie-knife I carry up my sleeves,
And if anyone should ask of me the reason why I wear them,
I'll tell him 'tis to guard myself from these garrotting thieves.

For a time garrotting attacks decreased in Dublin, but then 1895 saw a resurgence.[8] In October of that year, a gang of four assaulted a man on Thomas Street, and sporadic attacks were reported for a further decade or so before they petered out. In some instances, the victims were first plied with drink by their assailants, on the pretense of friendship. When one garrotter, Joseph Osborne, came before the Southern Police Court in September 1907, he had amassed a staggering record of thirty-one previous offences.[9]

Garrotting attacks were just one aspect of violent crime in Dublin. Gangs roamed the poorer parts of the city, particularly around Summerhill, where they threw stones at passers-by and quarrelled among themselves. Their arguments sometimes escalated into pitched street battles, such as those fought between the 'Boltonites', who hailed from the crowded inner-city tenements north of the Liffey, and their hated rivals the 'Georgians', who lived around South Great George's Street.[10]

In 1866 a Constable Penrose had a poker rammed into his eye when he peered through a Temple Bar keyhole during his hunt for a fugitive drunk. The injury kept him in hospital for six weeks. In 1855 a retired detective named Richard Doran was passing through Essex Street when he was recognised by a woman, whose jeers of derision drew a crowd. Gathering around the pensioner, they knocked him to the ground and kicked him brutally, one of them stabbing him in the wrist with a knife. Tenement dwellers frequently left barrels and other obstacles in darkened hallways on purpose so policemen might trip over them, and by the 1860s the beating of lone officers had become so frequent it had entered local parlance as the 'popular amusement'. Eventually, the activity became organised around a Dublin street gang known as the 'band boys', whose most notorious member was a powerfully built man named Francis Lacy. He served several prison terms, the longest of which lasted five years.[11]

In my own family there was apparently an aunt of my paternal grandmother's who, living around the turn of the twentieth century, learned to fight like a man and was able to hold her own. She once took on three policemen in Great Britain Street in a fight or 'lucky up'.[12]

In 1854 a Constable Dagg was brutally set upon when he attempted to break up a gang of street fighters at Islandbridge. When he followed them to a nearby house, they dragged him into a hallway and gave him another beating, leaving his uniform in shreds.[13] Policing in nineteenth-century Dublin was not for the timid.

5

ONE OF THE LAST DUELS IN IRELAND

It is the early hours, and the sun has not yet risen over Dublin Bay. Two men stand on Dollymount Strand, their shirtsleeves billowing like sails on the shore; one of them is wounded. They have just fought one of the last duels ever seen in the country. Beside them are two other gentlemen – their seconds, who are there to ensure fair play between the combatants.

In 1839 the fledging DMP force was called to deal with an unusual incident on Bull Island, near Clontarf in Dublin. The island is now well known for its long beach – the work of the famous Captain William Bligh, who surveyed Dublin Bay for the port authorities. It was also a popular place for duels, and arguments that began at the Theatre Royal were often known to finish on the shore.

Living in Dublin at that time were a Mr John O'Hara from Galway, who was treasurer to the crown solicitor, and a roguish barrister with the colourful name of Robert Napoleon

Finn.[1] Finn's father, a wealthy grocer from the west of Ireland, had enough wherewithal to send his son to the bar during the 1830s, and he soon made a name for himself in Dublin.[2] O'Hara had made a joke at the expense of Finn and, in keeping with the custom of those times, Finn immediately challenged him to a fight to the death. O'Hara refused to apologise, so they arranged to fight a duel at five o'clock in the morning – no doubt to escape the attention of the authorities.

We owe our knowledge of what happened next to a barrister named William Ireland, who owned both a country home in County Kildare and a townhouse on Gloucester (now Sean MacDermott) Street.[3] As a friend of one of the principals, he was invited to watch the action unfold on the lonely beach.

First, the two duellists took off their greatcoats and piled them on the sand. They then walked away from each other until they stood twelve paces apart.[4] One of the seconds stood between them and instructed them about how the duel was to proceed: 'The only signal will be the words "Ready – fire".'

The second then stood aside and the men faced each other, the wind whipping sand into their faces. Suddenly, the voice of the second cut through the tension: 'Fire!'

Neither combatant fired; the second had failed to give them advance notice with the word 'ready' and Finn was annoyed. He levelled his pistol at him.

'Be quiet, will you?' he said angrily. 'Do you want to have me accidentally shot?'

The second made another attempt to issue his instructions. He took a few paces back:

'Neither of you is to attempt to raise your pistol till I give the word "ready", nor to attempt to shoot till I give the word "fire".'

But this time Finn, who was now in a state of nervous agitation, only heard the word 'fire'. Without thinking he pulled the trigger, but his pistol was pointed downwards and he shot himself in the calf. O'Hara, thinking that Finn had fired at him, immediately took aim, but Finn hopped off as fast as he could on his wounded leg. 'For God's sake,' he cried, 'don't fire; it was all a mistake!' O'Hara did fire, however, and his bullet struck the ground close to Finn. Sand sprayed all over their coats.

Suddenly, the morning was filled with the thunderous sound of hooves. A pair of DMP constables appeared in a carriage, having received a tip that there was a duel at the North Bull, and they had warrants for the arrest of the entire party. Constable James Lowe had been on his 'bate' in Clontarf at four o'clock in the morning when he received word, and he had hastened to the scene with Constable 211C. On approaching the beach he heard shots fired, and a short time later he came across one of the seconds 'and a man dressed as a peasant' carrying the profusely bleeding Napoleon Finn in their arms. Meanwhile, Constable 211C saw two gentlemen running towards a covered car, so he gave chase and arrested them. Inside the vehicle, he found two boxes, each of which contained two cases of duelling pistols.[5]

The five men were bundled into the carriages, including Finn, whose leg dangled out the window to keep it cool, and they were brought back to Dublin. At Henry Street the men had to pay several hundred pounds to secure their bail, and a Surgeon Atkinson appeared as a witness to vouch that Finn had shot himself. He was able to remove the ball, which had lodged in his calf, 'exactly at the top of his boot, close to his ankle'.[6] The whole incident was enough to cause Pat Costello, a lawyer friend of the great Daniel O'Connell, to remark: 'Finn had gone to the Bull, got cow'd and shot the calf.'[7]

As a quirky postscript, duelling had all but died out in Europe until, in 1896, newspapers in Dublin (where cycle polo was becoming popular) reported that two young men had fought a duel on bicycles in Paris with drawn swords. The two

A duel on bicycles, fought on the Boulevard Ney in Paris.
(*Illustrated Police News*, 29 August 1896)

combatants had charged at each other from fifty paces apart. Failing to meet, they had wheeled about for a second attempt, but were thrown off their machines, along with their seconds, who had been peddling close behind. Incidents such as this, which provided fodder for the 'Tit Bits Inquiry' column, are believed to have inspired James Joyce's Ithaca chapter in *Ulysses*.[8]

Two decades later, there was a more fatal occurrence in Dublin. On 20 October 1923 *The Freeman's Journal* reported that a revolver duel had been fought in Finglas on bicycles, which resulted in the death of the head of Dublin's criminal investigation department.

6

RAINING CATS, DOGS AND OTHER ANIMALS

At first the hot air balloon rises over Dublin, but then the aeronaut begins to panic and his soaring ambitions are dashed. The machine is drifting seawards, out into the bay. There are decisions to make. He can drop his grappling iron, but it is sure to damage the new railway line. Instead he resolves to bring the balloon down for an emergency landing near the North Strand. He loses control as the basket skids into a field and is dragged towards a row of houses.

On 14 October 1844 Constable 153C dealt with a very unusual incident on Bayview Avenue, just off Dublin's North Strand. A hot air balloon, veering off course, had descended into a nearby field but unfortunately collided with a house in one of the city's newest suburbs. A short time earlier a chimney stack had caught fire, and the man who was on hand to tug the balloon's guide ropes could not stop the balloon from slamming into it, tearing part of a roof away in the process. Just then, the chimney fire ignited the balloon fabric:

A fearful explosion took place, and in an instant the immense globe, with all its appurtenances, was one dense volume of fire and smoke. The doors, windows, and railings of the houses in the immediate neighbourhood are much injured. Mr Hampton, in the confusion of the moment, had considerable difficulty in extricating himself from the car. He, however, providentially succeeded in throwing himself out just as the flames had reached the end near where he sat … the destruction of property is, notwithstanding, great, and appears to have made a very sensible impression upon his spirits; the balloon we have heard estimated at a value of over 600l.[1]

Realising the danger, the police constable managed to get inside the damaged house and he closed all the windows so the furniture inside could not catch fire.

The unlucky aeronaut was John Hampton, an Englishman and retired British navy officer who held the honour of being the first man to descend using a parachute – 10,000 feet over Cheltenham in 1838. On this occasion he was fortunate to escape the wreckage alive, as he had become tangled in the basket and ropes. Some passers-by pulled him free before the flames reached him.

Ireland's first balloon flight was made from the Rotunda Gardens, Dublin, on 4 February 1784. It was followed soon after by a manned flight, and by the early part of the nineteenth century a veritable balloon craze was underway. Police barrack grounds proved ideal for experimental flights, and trials with parachutes began almost immediately. From the outset, field tests were performed using live animals. In August 1785

French aeronaut Jean-Pierre Blanchard dropped a dog from his balloon near Lisle. It landed two miles away without sustaining any injury, but unfortunately the same could not be said for a fellow canine dropped over South Lambeth by one

PERILOUS - BALLOON - ASCENT. -

Ballooning could be risky. When a machine belonging to two French aeronauts reached 1,000 feet over Lille in June 1880, cold air caused the gas to condense and they plummeted earthwards. They were only saved when their anchor snagged in the branches of a tree. (*Illustrated Police News*, 12 June 1880)

Colonel Thornton. He also dropped out a cat, which made a more gradual descent, but used more than one of its nine lives when it landed unharmed in a tree. In 1817 a Dublin balloonist named Miss Thompson took a less ambitious approach by choosing to drop a parachute-wearing tortoise from her basket.

Four years after Hampton's balloon disaster, he redoubled his efforts with a new machine, triumphantly named *Erin Go Bragh*. In June 1849 it took off from the Rotunda Gardens into a sunny summer sky and this time came down safely in a meadow near Harold's Cross, after rising about a mile above the city. A force of police, under the supervision of an Inspector McGee, were there to control the crowd that had gathered to witness the spectacle.[2]

Shortly before Hampton retired, his name was connected with a series of bizarre parachute drops in Islington, London. The London *Daily News* of 13 August 1851 reported that:

On Monday evening last a balloon ascended from some gardens in the neighbourhood of Islington, and shortly afterwards, a parachute, freighted with a monkey, was separated, and, descending at a rapid rate, it fell in the garden of Mr Lovelock. Immense crowds of disorderly persons assembled, besieging the houses of applicants, and forced an entrance, which caused great alarm to the ladies and other inmates. Mr Lovelock, junr., proceeded to the garden, to take possession of the monkey, which was imprisoned in a cage. He was immediately attacked in a violent manner, and was severely injured by the parties who claimed the monkey and were anxious to obtain possession of it.

When the Islington case came to court, the finger of blame was levelled squarely at John Hampton. Some time later, however, it transpired that the devices used to transport the monkeys were actually unmanned balloons, none of which belonged to him.

In Dublin, balloon ascents were undoubtedly fascinating, but sometimes they caused problems for the DMP. In October 1845, for instance, a fight broke out at a balloon ascent at the Rotundo Gardens where a lottery was also being held to promote the event. Onlookers claimed that the promoter held the winning ticket in his hand, to the detriment of all the entrants who had no chance of winning. Three years later, as the revolutionary Young Ireland movement prepared to stage a revolution in Ireland, Hampton was prevented by the police in Dublin from going up in his balloon for fear that the machine might be used against the forces of the Crown.[3]

Yet despite such setbacks, John Hampton made over 100 ascents throughout his career, as well as seven death-defying parachute descents. It is unknown whether he, like his less scrupulous colleagues, ever put a monkey in a parachute, but what can be said with more certainty was that, at one time, he did make it rain cats and dogs.

7

POLICING IN ALL WEATHERS

In the foggy streets, it is difficult for the young constable to pinpoint his would-be attacker. He can't see more than a few feet in front of him; footsteps echo in all directions, and his bull's-eye lantern is useless. He peers cautiously into a murky alley; a chicken pecks the wet cobblestones in front of him. A hand pump, wraith-like, is his only point of reference. Groping ahead, one hand finds the whitewashed wall of a small thatched cottage. Somewhere in the distance, a horse whinnies, nervous in the deepening darkness.

'Now the city sleeps: wharves, walls, and bridges are veiled and have disappeared in the fog that has crept up from the sea; the shameless squalor of the outlying streets is enwrapped in the grey mist' – thus wrote Irish novelist George Moore of Dublin in *A Drama in Muslin*.[1]

Although Londoners consumed more coal per capita than their Irish counterparts, Victorian Dublin was still burdened with at least fifty days of charcoal-smelling smog each winter. Immortalised in the shanties of sailors who lay at berth, it could be more than just a nuisance, and during heavy spells the newspapers were peppered with reports of tragic drowning accidents in the Royal or Grand canals. Cross-Channel mail steamers were often delayed, and during such times the post office had to employ an army of special sorting staff and postmen to meet the bags when they arrived. A late-nineteenth-century seafaring ballad captured the spirit of the times:

Oh, the sun may shine through a Dublin fog,
And the Liffey run quite clear,
Or a p'liceman when wanted may be found,
Or I may forget my beer, my boys,
Or the landlord's quarter day,
But I can't forget my own true love,
Ten thousand miles away.[2]

Until the late 1860s there were no foghorns in Dublin Bay. Instead, the low chime of a bell could often be heard tolling in the dark swirl of the river mouth, calling to unseen ships. When such weather was at its worst, darkness fell early. The DMP constables marched out from their stations at nine o'clock. The public houses closed at eleven and, with the with-

The French caption reads *tenue des jours de pluie* or, in other words, an 'outfit for rainy days'.
(*Journal Universel*, 1867)

drawal of the horse-drawn omnibuses, the streets were usually deserted and silent. In the absence of any sign of bustling city life, the young recruits, known colourfully as 'Johnny Raws', were left to police Dublin's wheel-rutted laneways.

The police commissioners allowed the men to grow beards as protection against the cold and wet, and if the nights were particularly bad they might seek refuge in a cabman's shelter. During the 1850s an attempt was made to persuade the men to shave until, in a move worthy of today's hipsters, 400 constables subscribed to the 'beard movement': they signed a petition for permission to wear their beards because 'almost all, if not all, diseases of the respiratory organs, are in great part, if not altogether, caused by the practice which obtains of shaving off the beard'. Beards, they argued, were an adornment of nature, and by shaving them off they would be disfiguring themselves. At the same time, there was a 'moustache movement' among the various police forces in Britain. The Manchester papers reported that razors had been 'extensively discarded' there.[3]

Misguided connections were made between the so-called blue mist (ordinary fog) and cholera, but, regardless of the actual cause, chronic lung conditions were rife. *The Irish Times* regularly carried advertisements for Holloway's Pills, a quack remedy against 'suffocating fogs', and in 1849 the *Dublin Quarterly Journal of Medical Science* remarked that it was unfair to reduce the salaries of sick officers – those men who chose to walk their beat 'instead of skulking under an archway'.[4] Unable to afford the double blow of medical expenses and loss of pay, the men often chose to avoid the doctor, with lethal consequences.

In the case of one fatality, a physician remarked that the deceased 'had been quacking himself for some days'.[5] In 1896 a constable named Peter Carrigee went to arrest a man and was kicked violently. The attack brought on a haemorrhage which, according to a subsequent police report, 'accelerated already advanced tubercular disease'.[6]

During the early years of the force, Mercer's Hospital, near St Stephen's Green, was known as the DMP man's hospital. The Richmond Hospital, which was a House of Industry training hospital on the northside of the city, played a similar role. Its handbook for resident pupils specifically stated that 'in applications for admission as patients, members of the police force are to have a preference, and, in all present cases, vacancies must be made for them'.[7] In 1881, however, the Whitworth Hospital, which had been 'authorised to accommodate sick members of the force', refused to take them due to the sheer demand on its services.[8]

In homes across the city, mist seeped through casement sashes and under doors. In fact, it was so common an occurrence that Irish poet Donagh MacDonagh chose it as the first line of a poem: 'Fear, like a fog, slips in at every window'.[9] During such

Policemen insisted on keeping their beards, which helped insulate them in cold winter weather.
(*Journal Universel*, 1867)

nights Victorian Dublin was no safer than it had been when eighteenth-century bucks and cutthroats prowled the streets. Gas lamps cast eerie rainbow auras and, like the constable's bull's-eye lantern, were of little practical use. In 1868 a letter writer to the *Saunders Newsletter* complained that most of the lights on the north side of St Stephen's Green were broken, as were those along Kildare Street, Merrion Row and Baggot Street.[10]

When 'Fenian fever' descended on the city during the late 1860s, gunmen sometimes used the fog to move weapons or documents between houses, and there were a number of shooting incidents. Afterwards, assailants could make their escape relatively easily into the mist. For instance, when shots were fired at an inspector outside Sackville Place Station in November 1867, the police who tried to pursue the would-be assassin were confused by the fog, which distorted and amplified the sound of his running footsteps.[11] At other times, the force had to contend with opportunistic burglaries or jackbooted smugglers who hauled their cargos up the Tolka at Mud Island near Ballybough.

Thankfully, however, there were many other occasions when the policeman's duty was rather less onerous. The 'Granny's Corner' column, which began running in *The Irish Times* in the early 1900s, responded to correspondence from young readers. In one particularly moving letter, the columnist replied to a boy named Vincent as follows: 'It was lucky you met that invaluable policeman; a fog is the most bewildering thing in the world. I am sure you were glad to see the lights of home again – Your affectionate GRANNY.'[12]

8

GRAVE ROBBERS AND CROOKED CORONERS

Inside the walls of Glasnevin Cemetery a smell of sulphurous smoke rises; bullets strike the gravestones and blood colours the snowy ground. A desperate battle is being fought between a party of determined grave robbers and the cemetery watchmen. In the freezing night the battle reaches a desperate stage; the besieged protectors crouch low behind the granite stones. Suddenly a bell peals out. One of the watchmen has managed to sound the alarm. The police are on their way.

One of the last pitched battles between grave robbers, or 'sack-em-up' men, and the old city watch took place in Dublin's Glasnevin Cemetery one bitterly cold, snowy night in February 1830. A gentleman named Edward Barrett had died, and his friends – in the company of the graveyard's watchmen, who occupied the lookout towers – stayed on guard all night. The attack, which took place just a few years before the DMP was established, was the result of a shortage of bodies for Dublin's medical schools. Before the passage of the Anatomy Act in 1832, the only corpses that could be legally acquired were those of prisoners who had been executed. The demand was very high, however, and not just from the medical profession; dentists also needed the teeth from the dead for making dentures. (It is not surprising to discover that even today the old herb garden in Trinity College is littered with human bones.) In response, the wealthy purchased 'mort safes' – iron cages to cover their tombs.

The Anatomy Act of 1832 curtailed the trade in illegal bodies, as it then became possible for medical students to obtain corpses from the workhouses, or when relatives did not claim the deceased. However, it did not completely stop the practice, and the resurrectionists continued to ply their ghastly trade during the early years of the DMP. Alongside the city's nine public medical schools, there were also schools of anatomy in backyards, sheds and rooms of private houses.[1]

Bodies were still being procured illegally, and the problem was not confined to Dublin. In March 1839 a sailor in Cork encountered 'two skulls, one a male and the other a female's … in the river opposite Charles Bridge'. When he reported the discovery to Tuckey Street guardhouse, the police made a 'diligent search' and found 'some entrails about the same part of the river; the general opinion having been that the skulls were dissected ones'.[2] Cuban bloodhounds continued to patrol Glasnevin Cemetery after dark into the 1850s, until the city coroner, Dr Kirwan, had to fend them off with his back to a gravestone one night.

In January 1839 Constable 51B attended a tavern at Bow

Lane to investigate two suspicious-looking drunks. When he arrived, he found a 'wretched cadaverous-looking fellow' sitting there with a woman. She dropped a white bundle on the floor when the constable came in, then scrambled under a table to retrieve it. 'O my loaf!' she cried. 'What will I do for my loaf?' The policeman went to help her but was horrified to discover that the 'loaf' was actually a bloodied head and the sheet used to wrap it was covered with clotted blood. The officer then noticed that the man had a gravedigger's spade between his legs. The pub erupted in confusion and people began to shout: 'O, the bloody sack-'em-ups!'[3]

Constable 51B marched the pair off to the local station on College Street. Afterwards they searched the prisoners' garret room and discovered an old box filled with bones, including heads and arms held together by ligaments. A small parcel held over fifty winding sheets that had originally been used to wrap the stolen bodies.

A dramatic inquest at College Street Station ensued. It was revealed that the head was that of a disinterred child, and according to Sir James Murray, the inspector general of the schools of anatomy, the prisoners, John Neil and Bridget Byrne, were not licensed to bring bodies to the medical schools. It turned out that Byrne was the wife of a man who had already been sentenced to transportation for grave robbing. John Neil, on the other hand, was a noted grave robber. The police also tracked down a small boy whose job it was to go about the city and find out who had died. Every evening he would go back to the garret of Neil and Byrne to tell them what graveyard to

Grave robbing was profitable, but it could also be thirsty work. The image of a gluttonous resurrectionist in the background, pick-axe in hand, contrasts with the gravestone which reads 'sacred'. The cartoonist leaves his audience in no doubt that this gang are involved in an act of desecration. (*Resurrectionists* (1847), by Hablot Knight Browne)

go to. The boy was sent to live at the Mendicity Institution, a place for poor and indigent people on Usher's Quay.

Resurrectionists weren't the only ones causing the police

grief about dead bodies. Under the terms of the 1846 Coroner's Act, a coroner could order that a dead body be deposited in the nearest public house until an inquest could be held, and if the proprietor refused, he could be fined.

Beer cellars were quite cool and could slow the rate of decomposition. As time passed, it became common for publicans to keep marble tables in their cellars for autopsies. This legislation was not removed from the statute books until 1962, helping to explain the dual role of publican and undertaker that is still common, particularly in rural Irish towns, to this day.

But coroners were not always honest upholders of the law, and during the 1840s several were even arrested. In 1842 a coroner named Irwin was sentenced to seven years' transportation for forging a will and in March of the same year, another member of the profession was brought to court for assaulting a police constable in Dublin city centre.[4]

One of the most infamous cases that the DMP had to deal with involved a coroner named John Pasley and his medical attendant, surgeon R. B. Shanahan. The two men were convicted for submitting fictitious inquest paperwork on people who had died of natural causes, making it seem as though the deceased had expired in suspicious circumstances. This allowed them to hold an inquest from which they could earn a fee. Usually, if a coroner was called to examine a body, he recruited a local doctor to assist him, but Pasley always refused help from anybody except Shanahan. The DMP, who acted as middlemen in such cases (they arranged payment for the medical attendant), became suspicious when Pasley refused to pay a local doctor and insisted on the presence of Shanahan. Afterwards, the *Dublin Medical Press* remarked that a regular coroner's doctor was 'looked upon as a suspicious character'.[5]

Another story involving disreputable medical practitioners concerns a young man called Kinsella, who was on his way to work at the distillery on Marrowbone Lane on the morning of 11 March 1842. He was stopped at a bridge over the Grand Canal by a police constable, who ordered him to take his place as a juror at a forthcoming inquest. An old man had been found drowned in the canal. Kinsella tried to get out of the duty but was informed that the inquest would be very brief since there were no marks of violence on the corpse. He reluctantly agreed to go with the officer, but when he and his fellow jury members were ushered into the room where the corpse lay, Kinsella fell to his knees. 'My father!' he cried. 'We buried him on this day week in the Hospital Fields. He had no business in the canal and them old clothes never belonged to him!'

The doctor and the coroner tried to convince Kinsella that he was surely mistaken, but he remained adamant. An investigation followed, and it emerged that the coroner and the doctor had been disinterring recently buried bodies, dressing them up in old clothes and throwing them into the canal. Of course the bodies were always discovered, and if a corpse had been damaged by a passing barge, all the better – the coroner and the doctor were paid for the number of inquests they held, and the fee was doubled if a suspicious death was suspected and a post-mortem had to be conducted. The two professionals were duly convicted of conspiring to defraud.[6]

During the 1840s there was a spate of unusual 'drownings' in Dublin.
Unscrupulous coroners stood to benefit financially when a post-
mortem was held. (*Illustrated Police News*, 12 January 1884)

In 1869 there was an omnibus crash in Dublin. It is noteworthy that, according to *The Freeman's Journal*, the injured
were taken to Lawler's Pub to be treated rather than to the
nearby St Mary's Asylum.[7] When the editor of the newspaper
complained that the choice was inappropriate, the publican
defended himself in a strongly worded letter:

I beg to say that the body of Mrs Byrne was brought into my house by the direction of Dr Monks, and laid on the table of the taproom, where a large fire was burning. Blankets were at once brought down from the bed of my own family and wrapped around the body. Every possible effort was made to resuscitate her. My house was closed and business suspended while she remained there; everything required by the doctor and those in attendance were [sic] supplied by me.[8]

One of the most famous pubs in Dublin for the holding of inquests was the Templeogue Inn. Indeed, so many were held there that it went by the name of the Morgue, which is now its official title. The reason it received so many bodies is that it was situated near the old Dublin to Blessington steam tram line.

Besides public houses, hospitals were also sometimes used as coroners' courts when an inquest was required. One such was Mercer's Hospital, where Constable Patrick Keena, a member of the DMP, was brought after he was shot on the streets of the city in October 1867.

By then, Dublin hospitals had become responsible for all the city's judicial post-mortem inquiries, despite the corporation's motion in 1864 to erect one or two mortuary houses with adjoining jury rooms for 'the bodies of those persons who unhappily meet with death suddenly and violently'.[9] By 8 January 1866 a corporation yard in Fishamble Street was put into use for that purpose, but it had only been open a month when employees from a neighbouring firm complained about the 'annoyance being occasioned by the removal of bodies and from inquests held therein'.[10] Despite some hopes that a back entrance could be knocked through into Winetavern Street, the building was closed and the situation was not resolved.

A new city morgue was constructed in the early 1870s on Lower Abbey Street. This benefitted the DMP because the bodies of those who had died in suspicious circumstances could now be stored more easily for forensic analysis and the building was specially ventilated. The morgue was attached to the coroner's court and the only keys were held at College and Sackville Street police stations.[11] This stood in marked contrast to the old arrangement whereby inquests were held in various locations. The Marlborough Street morgue continued as such for many years until the premises was purchased, along with the adjacent Mechanics Institute, and opened by W. B. Yeats and Lady Gregory as the Abbey Theatre. Inevitably, the theatre attracted headlines such as 'The Muse at the Morgue', and during the renovation part of a human skeleton was discovered. This may have given rise to some of the theatre's ghost stories. Of the current, more modern theatre building, artistic director Tomás Mac Anna once said, 'no self-respecting ghost would be found dead in the place'.[12]

9

ZOZIMUS AND CONSTABLE 184B

Down the hill past Christ Church rings a familiar sound – a tap-tapping of metal on wheel-rutted cobbles. It comes from an iron-capped blackthorn stick gripped by a gaunt man dressed in a coarse frieze coat and brown beaver-skin hat. His name is Michael Moran, but he is better known to Dubliners as the blind street bard 'Zozimus'. He is destined to lock proverbial swords with one of the city's most eccentric policeman – the redoubtable Constable 184B.

By the 1820s Zozimus had become something of a celebrity in Dublin. He was a popular street balladeer and satirist who was born around 1794 in Faddle Alley off the Black Pitts. Blinded by illness as an infant, he displayed an astounding memory for verse and was nurtured in that talent by the musicians and poets of the Liberties. As one of his biographers later noted with pride, Moran could '*bate* them all hollow'.[1]

His nemesis was Constable 184B, a 'blue bottle' who proved to be the fly in his proverbial ointment. He arrested Zozimus on numerous occasions, unwilling to leave him alone. *The Freeman's Journal* of 7 September 1844 recounts how the bard was treated at the hands of this officer, who in his distinctive blue uniform, ordered him to 'move on and not obstruct the passage'.[2] Then, when Zozimus complained that it was a lucky spot and he had already made seven pence by standing there, the overzealous policeman seized him by the collar and dragged him off to the station (curiously, the newspaper still describes it as a 'watch house').

When the same officer also began to harass a *Freeman's Journal* reporter called Dunphy, the reporter and Zozimus decided to team up against him. Before long the constable found he could not move without some satirical piece being written about him, and he was waylaid by tourists on the streets. Of him, a journalist named Kearney wrote:

> How Proud Robert Peel must be of such a chap,
>
> He stands about five feet nothing in cap,
>
> And his name's immortalised by his friend Mr D[unphy],
>
> A statue must be riz to 184B.[3]

Eventually life became a daily misery for Constable 184B. Visitors to the city would seek him out and a crowd followed him wherever he went; he couldn't take a step or blow his nose without a loud cheer.

Zozimus, who was described by many as having a deep, booming voice, was called after the piece for which he was best known – a long narrative poem by the Bishop of Raphoe titled *The Life of Saint Mary of Egypt*. Unable to enter the Church of the Holy Sepulchre due to a supernatural force, a seductress spends the next forty-seven years wandering the desert. As she nears death, God dispatches a bishop named Zozimus to give her Holy Communion and a lion is sent to dig her grave.

The poem formed only part of Moran's repertoire, however. Each morning he had the newspaper read to him. Afterwards he would say, 'That'll do. I have me meditations.'[4] Then he would spin a piece of satire out of whatever story was most current – a fact that caused musician Luke Kelly to categorise him as 'a musical newspaper man'.[5]

With his rhymes consigned to memory, Zozimus roamed all over Dublin. He went as far afield as Donnybrook Fair, but in general his favourite haunts were Dame Street, Capel Street, Grafton Street, Sackville Street, Henry Street, and Carlisle and Essex bridges. Once he had chosen his 'lucky spot' he would cry: 'Gather round me boys, gather round poor Zozimus, yer friend. Boys, am I standin' in a puddle, am I standin' in wet?'

'Ah no, yer not,' they would reassure him. 'Yer in a nice dry place. Go on with "St Mary". Go on with "Moses".'[6]

If he was satisfied, he would spread out his arms as if to catch all passers-by and then give a great shrug of his shoulders and say:

Ye sons and daughters of Erin, attend,
Gather round poor Zozimus, yer friend;
Listen, boys, until yez hear
My charming song so dear ...[7]

By the 1820s Zozimus had become a household name, but although his fame was enough to provide him with the essentials of life, it never made his fortune and the DMP continued to harass him wherever he went. Nevertheless, his family were well fed, and he earned enough money to provide mutton chops from Blackhall Place. Each evening, he returned home to the humble room he shared

The Ballad Singer

As a street entertainer, Zozimus attracted many imitators and provided inspiration for those who came after him. (*Illustrated London News*, 29 October 1881)

with his wife. He was prone to outbursts of temper and once flung a bowl of stirabout at her in a fit of pique. When she died, he married a widow named Mary Curran.

One of the most intimate insights into the life of Zozimus comes from Patrick McCall. The biographer describes how a lad is sent by his aunt to buy a ballad from the blind poet in which his opinion of the local police force features prominently. Joining him on his return journey from Smithfield Market, the boy climbs the hill at Christ Church with him. The fatigued Zozimus calls into Curran's around the vicinity of Michael's Hill and revives his spirits with some 'whiskey droppings'; the dregs of spilt drink left on a tray (and a cheap alternative to buying a bottle). A short time later, he raises the latch at his Cole's Alley home and enquires:

'Where a' ye, Paddy?'

'Under de table, Daddy!'

'An' where's your mammy?'

'Gone to de fountain wid the taypot!'

'Gone to de fountain wid the taypot? – Ah, just as Masther Mike said: "Moran, it's all the fault o' your taypot!"' (Zozimus had been complaining to Mike, his assistant, about the poor quality of his tea.)

Soon his wife returns with the teapot, but Zozimus berates her: 'Mary, dear, I'm disthressed to think that the charakter of Masther Mike's Bohay should suffer through an unscientific application on your part!':

The proper way to make your tay
Is, when the wather's b'iled,
Take your pot, an' make it hot,
If not, the tay is sp'iled!

Then Zozimus got down to business. 'Mary, dear, this boy here has a message from Miss Wall of Back Lane; the lady I meet comin' from the twelve o'clock mass in Adam and Eve's – God bless her! She's wantin' Billy's Downfall (a ballad poem) for a friend who's lavin' town this evenin'.'

In the poem, Zozimus distanced himself from having anything to do with vandalising the equestrian statue of King

William of Orange (King Billy) on College Green. He did, however, reserve a special ire for the police, whom he referred to as 'peelers', and in one memorable verse he recalled his various encounters with the old city watch:

> By peelers, pig-stealers, and all dirty dealers,
> I vow that my oath is both honest and true.
> I owe spite to no man, high Dutchman or low man;
> With watchmen, when tipsy, I might have a brawl,
> But plotting 'gainst dead men, or knocking down lead men …
> I ne'er had a hand in King Billy's downfall.[8]

'But Sol Kelly got the last one in the place!'

'Indeed – Paddy, go downstairs an' tell Sol Kelly I want him.'

After a few minutes, Sol Kelly made his appearance: 'Good morning, Mick,' he said. 'What sort ov a market had ya?'

'I thank ye for the enquiry, Sol. The ethaireal thunder of Dan's eloquence in Mahony's last week has greatly affected the market for the better. It has entered the sowls of the min and stirred the pockets of the wimen. Ah, Sol, when I come to the end ov the third verse:

> O'Gorman Mahon will back brave Dan,
> We care not for the college, oh!

the air becomes balmy with the sighs of sweet defiance, an' I can hear the rhinos in the pockets of the crowd strugglin' for freedom to execute a thransmissive gallop.'

There was a rap at the door; Sol was wanted.

'Before you go, Sol,' Zozimus said, 'I want the ballid on Billy's Downfall ye got from Mary: it was the only one left.'

As a street entertainer, Zozimus attracted many imitators. One of these was a man named Rogers. At supper one night in a local tavern, some friends wagered that he could not appear on the streets dressed as Moran. They reasoned that the crowd would surely be able to tell the difference. Determined to prove them wrong, Rogers set out for Capel Street Bridge the following evening and took up a position near the real Zozimus. Soon, a puzzled crowd gathered around them.

'Good Christians,' Rogers protested. 'Is it possible that any man would mock the poor dark man like that?'

'Who's that?' Zozimus said. 'It's some impostherer.'

'Begone, you wretch,' Rogers replied. 'It's you'ze the impostherer. Don't you fear the light of heaven bein' sthruck from your eyes for mocking the poor dark man?'

'Saints and angels,' Zozimus protested, 'is there no protection against this? You're a most inhuman bla'guard to try to deprive me of my honest bread this way.'

The crowd began to murmur and, as the word spread, the bridge thronged with people, all eager to witness the unfolding scene.

'Is it possible that none of yez can know me?' Zozimus protested. 'Don't yez see it's *myself*, and *that's* someone else?'

Rogers ignored him and began to tell the story of Moses's Nile journey into the bulrushes. Zozimus fought back with his *The Life of Saint Mary of Egypt*. Then, just as the situation reached fever pitch, the impersonator admitted his trickery. As a sign of good faith, he even put a few shillings into Zozimus's hand before he was carried off in triumph by his friends.[9]

Zozimus's Dublin was one of small, narrow streets away from the main thoroughfares, and although the Wide Streets Act had allowed for the clearing away of a large swathe of the medieval city, leaving Parliament Street, Sackville Street and Dame Street in its wake, there were still hundreds, thousands perhaps, of single-storey mud cottages where chickens could be found pecking in yards. During the course of his life, Zozimus lived in several places after Faddle Alley, including Pump Alley off Camden Street and latterly 14½ Patrick Street. This forgotten city is perhaps best captured in the series of *Darkest Dublin* photographs that were reproduced some years ago in Christian Corlett's superb book.

It was in the main streets, however, where the blind bard could attract the most attention and consequently the best of the day's takings. Every day of the week he had a different stand: the old Carlisle Bridge, old Essex Bridge and Smithfield. P. J. McCall, who wrote a lovely pen portrait of the man, added that the last time his father saw Zozimus, he was standing at the junction of Grafton Street and St Stephen's Green. Another favourite haunt was Patrick Street, near to his home, where he regaled the market crowd on Saturdays: 'Gather round me, boys! Gather round me! Well, yez all know Saint Patrick was born in Bull Alley!'

'More power, Zozimus!' cry the street urchins. 'Yer the rale heart o' the rowl! Tip us the T. B. C.! There's no damp on the taypot! That ye may never die!'

Then the old man gets angry with them and waves them away with his stick: 'You see here, me rowdy customers, if yez don't lave off yer skylarkin' I'll cut the ground from under some of yez!' Then he starts:

Saint Patrick was a gentleman, he came of dacent people,
He built a church in Dublin Town and on it put a steeple!

On one occasion, Zozimus was challenged by a gentleman on Carlisle Bridge to rhyme the word *bridge* for sixpence. Without missing a beat, the bard said:

Ah, kind Christian! Do not grudge
The sixpence promised on the brudge.

But things did not always go so well for the blind bard whose 'recimitations' sometimes caused an obstruction on roads and footpaths, and he was often arrested by the redoubtable Constable 184B. In late October 1844 he was called to break up an argument between Zozimus and a poet named Timothy Casey who, the former claimed, was nothing more than an imposter and a 'booby'. When Zozimus told Casey that it was well known that *he* was a man of genuine poetic ability who would live as long as Homer, Casey quipped that 'the only point in which Zozimus resembled Homer was in his blindness'.[10]

By then, 184B had attracted some fame in his own right

and he was certainly quite a character. He lived with his aunt, and in his spare time he courted a servant girl named Bridget Molloy from Windmill Lane. He liked to take his annual holidays in Dundrum, which in those days was quite rural and, for the benefit of his health, he lived to travel the roads on a hired donkey. On at least one occasion, he turned up in court sporting a monocle in his right eye.[11] In the police court, he was given to colourful turns of phrase. On one occasion, he shut the defendant up with the words: 'Silence, tinker, or I'll strike terror into your kettle-mending soul'.[12] In July 1844 his efforts to subdue a mad dog named 'Jowler' on Sackville Street brought him to public notice when *The Freeman's Journal* reported that he:

> … gave fierce chase, and after leaping over innumerable turf-kishes, apple stands, little children, old women, and a variety of similar obstacles which happened to obstruct his course, succeeded in overtaking Jowler at the corner of Great Britain street, and by a well-directed blow upon the forehead deprived the animal of life.[13]

Afterwards, the policeman walked back up Sackville Street, holding the dog's body by the tail and when he reached Carlisle (now O'Connell) Bridge, he flung it unceremoniously into the River Liffey. He was frequently made the butt of jokes, mainly as a result of his treatment of street balladeers, who lampooned him mercilessly in verse. As a result, Dubliners felt that they could freely harangue him whenever they chose to do so. On one occasion, a drunk named Mulligan (who he later hauled off to a police cell) asked him whether his mother knew he was out patrolling on Westmoreland Street at that hour of the night.[14]

That did not dissuade the constable from taking Zozimus into College Street Station, however. When the bard was arrested at Cole's Lane market in October 1840, he later protested:

> Yer worship, I love my country, she's dear to my heart. And am I to be prevented from writing songs in her honour, as Tommy Moore, Walter Scott, aye, or Homer, have done for theirs, and of singing them after the manner of the ancient bard, save that I haven't a harp to accompany my aspirations?[15]

It is evident from contemporary newspaper reports that Zozimus used the courtroom as a public stage, and in many instances the presiding magistrates were quite sympathetic to him, sometimes alluding to his talent as a street poet. All of this was, of course, eagerly noted down by journalists in the courtroom, who captured the blind bard's excellent and often highly inventive command of language.

In December 1841 184B brought Zozimus before the police court in College Street with some friends of his; they had all been found drinking in a lodging house in Exchequer Street at two o'clock in the morning. The following is a transcript of the conversation that ensued:

Mr Tyndall   Well, what can you say to the charge made against you?

Zozimus   I humbly thank your worship. You see, the nature of
            my avocations is numerous and varied, and they are
            carried on in different portions of the fair demain
            of this ancient city – (laughter). I am compelled
            to remain out at night in order to keep the penny
            stirring, and my residence is far, far away, in the
            Liberty; I was perambulating the streets last night,
            and, as the wind blew keenly, it was bitter cold, so
            I stepped into the house – for, oh, that house is open
            to the houseless child of want! – (laughter). But
            I assure your worship, with all possible respect, that
            I did not taste one drop o' de dew at all.

Policeman   They had spirits on the table, and I heard that man
            singing and drinking to the health of the other
            persons before I went in.

Zozimus   That's a pure mistake, I do confess, your worship,
            that I spoke rather high on the subject of native
            manufacture; and sure, if I took a drop to warm the
            inward and outward man, why where's the harm?[16]

By the end of 1845 Zozimus was seldom encountered in public.
When last seen on South Great George's Street, he was unable
to talk and he just placed a finger to his mouth whenever anyone
tried to speak to him. In March 1846 Reverend Farrell from St
Nicholas of Myra Church was asked to make a sick call to his
home. He arrived to find the poet prostrate on a straw pallet in
a room crowded with ballad singers, and Zozimus died there
shortly afterwards, on 3 April.

Some time earlier, the body of his friend Stoney Pockets (so named because he kept pebbles in his pockets to settle his dizzy spells) had been plundered by the resurrection men from Merrion Churchyard. As a result, Zozimus had a mortal fear of grave robbers. In the interests of safety, his friends arranged to have him interred in the walled cemetery at Glasnevin.

On the day of the funeral, the assembled friends grumbled about their lack of a 'rosner', or glass of spirits, to warm them. 'It's cruel cold, isn't it,' said one. 'We'll all be as stiff as the corpse when we get to the berrin-ground.' 'Bad cess to him,' grumbled another. 'I wish he held out another month till the weather got dacent.' At that someone took out a bottle of whiskey and offered to pass it around. Things were looking up until a spring on the hearse broke, tumbling the mourners headlong into each other. As they tried to regain their composure, the bottle of whiskey smashed on the cobbles – a fact to be mourned almost as much as the dead man.

Considering the extent to which the mourners, most of them street entertainers, had been harassed and harangued by the police, they were fortunate to be allowed to mourn the passing of their friend without interference. Unfortunately, the same could not be said of Constable 184B. The ghost of the blind street poet continued to haunt him after his death. After Zozimus had been laid to rest, a dispute arose at a Protestant church meeting in Dublin. One of those present advised that 184B be sent for at once. 'Didn't he take Zozimus by himself,' another said. The meeting room erupted in laughter. The constable could not salvage his damaged reputation. Eventually he was removed from the force, and for many years afterwards there was no 184B in the College Street division.[17]

Remarkably, the grave of Zozimus had no headstone until the Dublin City Ramblers paid to have one erected during the 1960s. Today, it can still be found in the 'poor ground' of the cemetery (AG 30 South). The epitaph reads:

> My burying place is of no concern to me,
> In the O'Connell Circle let it be,
> As to my funeral, all pomp is vain,
> Illustrious people does prefer it *plain*.

10

THE LAST KING OF MUD ISLAND

Police constable 88C, being sworn, said that having heard of the riot in Bayview Avenue, he took a hack car and hastened to it; when he got there, he saw several of the mob clapping McDonnell on the back and crying out 'hurrah for the king of Mud Island'. – The Freeman's Journal, *2 October 1838*

By the early 1800s, Mud Island, bounded on one side by the North Strand and on the other by Ballybough, had gained a notorious reputation and in times to come, it would cause trouble for the DMP. It was unsafe for agents of the law to enter, particularly after nightfall, and when a gentleman reported that he, his wife and their two children were assaulted with stones when passing through the area in July 1825, the police at Henry Street informed him that 'the inhabitants of Mud Island were such people that no stranger ought to go near the neighbourhood'.[1] In September 1843 when a police constable was called to remove a prisoner from a house, 'a crowd collected and commenced a desperate attack on him; they tore his clothes into pieces and battered his body almost to jelly'.[2]

An oft-quoted local saying was 'sure it's a wise man never saw a dead wan', and by day it was not unheard of to find the corpses of customs men or police officers floating on the incoming tide.[3]

Mud Island was presided over by its own 'king', the last of whom was Christopher McDonnell, who was born around the year 1798. The whereabouts of his baptismal record is unknown, but the Glasnevin Cemetery register gives his approximate age at time of death in 1852.[4] He is described by the *Industries of Dublin* as 'of low stature but very powerful'.[5] He married at least twice and was father to six children – three girls and three boys. In contrast to the small, half-acre holdings farmed by his neighbours, his Mud Island homestead was a substantial plot of three Irish acres located at the end of what is now King's Avenue. It comprised offices and a garden, as well as a crop of osier or willow trees, which extended as far as the modern-day railway embankment at Clonmore Terrace. Running eastwards was a fowl yard surrounded by a paling as well as a sixteen-foot-wide 'stable lane'. Wilson's *Modern Plan of the City and Environs of Dublin* from 1798 depicts a small, well-organised complex of buildings towards the Ballybough end of Mud Island that roughly corresponds to this holding.[6]

The McDonnells worked to exploit the land's best natural asset – sand. This was sold to the building trade, and a number of pits were dug for that purpose; for local children it was 'an esteemed joy' to get a jaunt in one of the king's sand carts. Besides sand carting, local people were engaged in various other legitimate occupations. They were dairy farmers, jarveys car operators, carters and porters for passengers disembarking from ships at the nearby port. There were also several turf yards in the area, the fuel carted from the Dublin Mountains for sale locally. Island women sold apples at the turnpike gates or made articles of clothing at home. Beggars also congregated in the vicinity.[7]

On 20 November 1826 *The Freeman's Journal* reported the 'apprehension of a Mud Island Chief' – a highwayman named Richard Lynagh for whom a warrant had been out for at least seven months.[8] All of the early kings had been highwaymen, many of whom were quite charismatic in their own way, but McDonnell, who came after them, broke the mould on account of his profession as a house builder. Nevertheless, he still managed to attract a considerable local following. He was said to carouse with 'Collier the Robber' and the duellist Bryan 'Bully' Maguire at the Ballybough Cockle Hall, where the famous Dublin Bay variety was a stewed speciality.[9] His notoriety was such that two men arrested in 1837 and 1847 for highway robbery and stealing gave 'McDonnell' and 'Christopher McDonnell' as aliases.[10]

As king, Christopher McDonnell was said to have exercised tight control over his neighbours. In 1853 *The Dublin University Magazine* recalled that when a 'tenant' was in arrears, McDonnell simply walked into his house and took whatever he could lay his hands on to make up the value of the rent.[11] Legend has it that when he was outbid for a house in the new suburb of Drumcondra, he exacted an unusual revenge:

That winter's evening when darkness fell found an army, literally of the island men, with their chief at their head, surrounding the house in dispute, now empty and deserted. The place was a lonely spot in those days and the invading force, working I suppose by the light of bonfires, demolished the house to the foundations before the sun rose the next morning … when McDonnell sat down to his breakfast, he had his opponent's house in small pieces, deposited safely in the heart of his island citadel.[12]

A fictitious account of a tar-and-feather operation supervised by the king appeared in an 1862 edition of *The Illustrated Dublin Journal*, but it has all the elements of a real event. At the very least, it shows the extent to which Mud Island had begun to grip the public imagination:

The tar brush was most vigorously and unsparingly applied by half a dozen willing operators, who speedily covered the body corporate of poor Horseman [a city official] with a dense bituminous coat, his entreaties for mercy and forbearance being interrupted by the casual introduction of the loaded tar brush into his gaping mouth … The execution of the Mud Island sentence terminated by Horseman, tarred and feathered as he was, being drummed out of the King's territories beyond the Spring Garden frontier, with all the ignominy considered to be due to a spy and an informer.[13]

On 14 November 1817 Christopher McDonnell's proprietorship of Mud Island changed abruptly. On that date John Stratford, third earl of Aldborough, 'made or impressed to be made' between them an indenture of lease to cover all the 'dwelling houses, tenements and buildings erected and built thereon', thus relegating the king to the status of a tenant on the earl's land.[14]

Aldborough's seizure of the territory was probably spurred on by the passing of the 1801 Enclosure (Consolidation) Act, which in effect removed the right of ordinary people to graze their livestock on common land, and it effectively changed the status of Mud Island from a commons to that of a leasehold acreage, an enclosed private property. A lengthy memorial goes on to name various tenants, each of whom required McDonnell to enter into a reciprocal arrangement with them. That made him a kind of middleman for small parcels of land scattered throughout Mud Island.[15] The forced nature of the tenancy agreement between the Earl of Aldborough and Christopher McDonnell goes a considerable way towards explaining the king's unwillingness to engage with the city authorities over the next thirty years or so. He consistently refused to pay his rent, and around 1820 a party of bailiffs, accompanied by soldiers, arrived to arrest him. They set off back towards the city with their prisoner, but:

In a few minutes time … the news spread through McDonnell's demesne and his loyal and loving subjects, hastily arming themselves, hurried on the tracks of the audacious enemy, whom they soon overtook and, confident in their hundreds, fiercely charged the soldiers who were compelled to fire again and again killing and wounding many of their pursuers, notwithstanding the fact that the island men had few firearms [they were mainly armed with their usual weapon, a four-inch chisel screwed onto a pike staff].[16]

Finding themselves outnumbered on Portland Row, the soldiers took shelter in Aldborough House. By then the old mansion had long since been abandoned and was occupied by the languishing Feinaglian Institute – a preparatory school for young ladies. Amid a shower of stones, the soldiers managed to partially close the wooden gates, and in the melee the king was found hiding in the porter's lodge in the courtyard. When he had the presence of mind to utter his trademark 'cock crow', the islanders charged the gates, 'chisel pike clashing with bayonet and then, in a few moments, the king was rescued and borne back Tolka-wards in triumph'.[17]

Contemporary newspaper accounts suggest that such activity was commonplace in Mud Island during the early nineteenth century. On 25 July 1826, for instance, *The Freeman's Journal* reported that the previous Sunday night a prison escort commanded by Peace Officer McDowell had been set upon by a party of 'Mud Island rangers'. Two members of the mounted horse patrol named Canterbury and O'Neill attempted to intervene, but the 'mob' followed them a considerable distance along the road, 'discharging on them showers of stones by which O'Neill's horse was knocked down a precipice of upwards of ten feet'.[18]

On 1 September 1832 the *Morning Chronicle* carried news of another sensational incident. A large mob of islanders led by Christopher McDonnell was reported to have attacked a barred and bolted property in Phillipsburg Avenue, armed with crowbars and other weapons. The premises had been seized by the sheriff's bailiff. Eventually 'a detachment of the boys' managed to gain entry, dislodging the bailiffs and accompanying troops, who retreated back towards the city. Later, a command of horse police was dispatched from the newly opened DMP headquarters in Exchange Court. They managed to dislodge the 'Royal McDonnell' and his followers, who escaped with difficulty, leaving the 'heir presumptive' – the king's eldest son Luke – to the mercy of the police. Luke was escorted to St Werburgh's watch house, where he spent the night. Contemporary newspaper depictions of the raiders as 'rangers' may have served as the basis for two of Pat Kinsella's Dublin music hall numbers in the late nineteenth century – the 'Mud Island Fusiliers' and 'Ballybough Bridge Brigade'.

During the Christmas season McDonnell liked to attend various theatres in the city, but he always went accompanied by an armed guard in case he was arrested by the police or attacked by one of his many creditors. He carried a blackthorn stick and on at least one occasion was discovered to have about him 'a detonating pistol loaded with three balls and percussion caps'.[19]

On many occasions the king deliberately antagonised the city authorities. *The Freeman's Journal* of 3 August 1831 reports on an unusual summons issued against him by Robert Torrens, judge of the Common Pleas. The judge's dog had wandered into Mud Island, where he was given refuge by the king, but when a coachman was dispatched to retrieve the animal, McDonnell refused to hand it over. Torrens sent a bailiff to Mud Island to serve a court order to the king, but on arrival he was attacked and the paper was taken from him. *The Freeman's Journal* of 9 November 1831 reports that:

> His assistant was struck violently with a shovel by Mr McDonald [*sic*]; and several other violent persons having congregated, the assistant or bailiff was compelled to eat the order; he was beaten again, and, in conclusion, as if to clothe him in the livery of his Majesty, the poor bailiff was dragged through the puddle and nearly suffocated. Thus, they were not only deprived of the original order, but also nearly killed.[20]

Judge Torrens's dog wandered into Mud Island and became the property of the king. (Courtesy of Alamy Stock Photo)

The destruction of the paper presented a particular legal difficulty for the authorities. Legally, a case could not proceed to court unless an order had been served to a defendant, and as a result the city grand jury threw out the bills that had been drafted. The remedy was to apply for a 'substitution of service' that would permit Judge Torrens's representative to simply affix a copy of the order to the door of McDonnell's home. A 'writ of assistance' was also applied for because it was deemed impossible to serve the defendant without help. These measures were accepted, but when the case came to court the king sent his nephew in his stead. He claimed that the dog had been in the king's possession for at least a year and a half which, under common law rights of ownership, effectively made the animal his. Once again, McDonnell had made a farce of the law.

A National Archive will abstract book shows that Christopher McDonnell died on 10 June 1852, leaving effects under £20 to his widow, Mary.[21] *The Nation* of 20 January 1855 added that 'it is very well that the late King of Mud Island is not alive; if he were, he would very properly claim the sovereignship of the whole city'. McDonnell was buried in a pauper's plot at Prospect Cemetery, Glasnevin.[22]

Two years later, his daughter Jane married a local tradesman named Robert Skinner. On 27 August 1864 his son Samuel died a bachelor at his home in Eccles Street. The family continued to live in Ballybough for many years afterwards and remained residents of King's Lane until at least 1870, when McDonnell's daughter Bridget married for a second time.[23] Thus, the claim by Dublin historian, Dillon Cosgrave, that 'there is no ground for asserting that King's Lane, now Avenue, was the royal residence' is refuted.[24] By the end of the nineteenth century, Mud Island and its king had been all but forgotten, remembered only in local folklore and music hall ballads.[25]

11

AN APACHE ATTACK ON PARNELL SQUARE

An Apache, dressed for war, gallops in pursuit of his enemy. Resplendent in his warrior's headdress of eagle feathers, he appears to be much taller than he really is. Cornering his quarry at last, he dismounts, draws his knife and attacks.

Such a scene would have been familiar to my father and his friends, who, growing up in the 1940s, watched Westerns in the 'fourpenny' rush at the Mayro Cinema. Sitting on long benches, they cheered for the cowboys and jeered whenever the 'Indians' appeared. They used to sing the following song, to the tune of 'Davy Crockett', which is worth quoting here because I have never seen it in print elsewhere:

Davy, Davy Crockett,
The king of the wild frontier,
Born in a pillar-box in Francis Street,
Brought to the Tivo so he knew every seat,

AN APACHE ATTACK ON PARNELL SQUARE

Got himself a haircut for one and three
And killed all the fleas with DDT ...[1]

What is surprising is that during the late nineteenth century, there was a *real* Apache attack in Dublin, long before celluloid made its first appearance. It happened on Dublin's Parnell Square in December 1892, and one of the first people on the scene was Constable 178C. He usually walked the beat up and down Sackville Street, around the market area and the environs of the square. He appears in the records on a number of occasions before this attack, some of the incidents more dramatic than others. A few years previously he had brought a man to Jervis Street Hospital after he was knocked down on Sackville Street by a hackney car.[2] In October 1888 his name was mentioned in connection with an unusual collision between the drunken operator of a 'tricycle milk machine' and a cab on Henry Street.[3] On another occasion he had to run after a woman who had stolen twelve pounds of ham and bacon from a butcher's on Moore Street. One of the most serious incidents he ever had to deal with was in September 1881, while attempting to arrest a butcher's porter on Moore Street for 'profane language', when he was boxed and kicked and the prisoner was rescued by the crowd. During that same incident, his colleague, Constable Daly, was stabbed to death by another porter with a large butcher's knife.[4]

Thus, Constable 178C had certainly experienced his fair share of knife crime when he encountered Running Wolf on Parnell Square in 1892. Mexican Joe's Wild West Show had just ended for the evening at the Rotunda and, as usual, it was followed by a procession around the square of gunslingers, Native Americans on horses and other exotic characters to help advertise the show.

Two bill posters had been sent to the Rotunda Gardens with a horse and cart to take some timber away. One of the men, Joseph Bryan, told his colleague, 'There's one of the Red Indians.' He followed the procession and, according to some accounts, started to taunt the participants. The police constable arrived on the scene just as Running Wolf, tired of the comments, jumped off his horse and punched Bryan in the head. He then stabbed him through the hand, knocking him against the railings.

When Running Wolf appeared afterwards in Capel Street Police Court, he was described by *The Freeman's Journal* as a 'brawny Apache Indian of Mexican Joe's Wild West Show'.[5] Wolf (whose real name was Charles Jefferson) took the stand in ordinary European clothes. His long, straight hair hung down his back and he spoke almost no English. Standing behind him were a number of his companions, all dressed in their show costumes. It was surely one of the strangest sights ever to grace a Dublin courtroom. The injured party, Joseph Bryan, took the stand, his hand wrapped in bandages. He explained how the 'Indians' had left the Rotunda Gardens the previous evening to advertise the show on horseback and Running Wolf had launched a savage and unprovoked attack. He told the judge that he was now unable to work and that he had to be treated in hospital.

Speaking through an interpreter, the Native American denied this. Although he accepted that there had been a confrontation, he claimed that Bryan's injury was the result of his falling back onto the railings of the Rotunda. The interpreter explained that Running Wolf had simply tried to calm his horse with the word *whoa* – a Native American word new to Irish ears – and for some reason Bryan had seen fit to make some disparaging remarks. Arriving on the scene, Constable 178C had to calm the excited performers who gathered around the two men.

Whatever the truth of the matter, the incident did little to dampen the enthusiasm of Dubliners for Mexican Joe's Wild West Show, and it might even have helped to publicise it. The *Evening Herald* of 21 December 1892 ran with the headline 'Alleged Stabbing by a Redskin', and other papers followed suit. Night after night, crowds flocked to the Rotunda Theatre. The spectacle proved so popular that extra dates were added, with the full schedule extending to Mondays, Wednesdays and Saturdays.

For two magical hours, the audience watched as an array of artistes graced the sawdust ring. They included a Miss Martini, who engaged in some clever shooting by leaning backwards and firing at a target over her head while sitting in a chair, and the acrobatic Texas rangers, who showed their ease in the saddle by picking up handkerchiefs from the ground while riding at speed. Such displays were interspersed with set pieces fought between cowboys and Indians – all foreshadowing the cinematic Western.

The man behind all this was Mexican Joe, otherwise known as 'Colonel' Joe Shelley. Encouraged by the success of William 'Buffalo Bill' Cody, he had set sail from Baltimore in July 1887, albeit on a much smaller scale than his famous rival. He appeared with his entourage in Edinburgh, and when the show reached Earl's Court in London, it was sketched by Irish artist Jack B. Yeats. Unlike Bill's, the troupe crossed over to Belfast and Dublin in the autumn and winter of 1892–93.

Shelley, decked in the gallant trim of a Confederate Army captain, recounted numerous tales of hair-raising adventure to anybody who would listen. On one occasion he even claimed that he had been captured by the Apaches himself.

But there was a more sinister side to Joe's show. Although

Running Wolf tries to murder Mexican Joe.
(*Illustrated Police News*, 21 January 1888)

Running Wolf and his fellow Native Americans were supposedly looked after very well, there was considerable dissatisfaction among the troupe. On 7 January 1888 the *Era* reported that Wolf had 'attempted the Colonel's life on several occasions' and that when he was in drink, it took the strength of the whole company to hold him down. When Jefferson's wife gave birth to a baby daughter on 27 January 1892, the child was promptly put on show as the 'Indian Papoose'. Everything, it would seem, had a price for Mexican Joe.

Running Wolf and his companions were billed as Apache or Sioux, but in truth they were neither. They were most likely described as such because anything else would have confused a European audience. Separated from their families and forced to wear strange clothes for a dollar a day, many were homesick. They continued to attract glances from passers-by whenever they went out on the streets of Dublin, but they had no further trouble with the police.

Mexican Joe's show at the Rotunda ended in January 1893. It continued to tour in England until it was overtaken by commercial failure at Barnsley, Yorkshire in 1894. By then the era of the great Wild West Show was at an end. It is uncertain what became of Running Wolf, but what can be said with certainty is that in the great tradition of the American frontier, he was a man who refused to be tamed.

12

THE
TRAM-RACING
STILT WALKER

'Roll up! Roll up! All the fun of the circus for one remaining night only. You sir – you look as though you may be a gentleman of fine and discerning sensibilities. Why then, look no further than Ginnett's Circus on Earlsfort Terrace; all life is here, sir. See our amazing and stupendous acrobats; marvel at our elephants; see the amazing stilt-walking Rossini. Yes sir, Ginnett's has everything under one roof to refresh body and soul.'

In 25 March 1886 several police constables were dispatched from College Street Station on an unusual traffic assignment. Early that morning, an advertisement had been circulated around the city:

FOR THIS NIGHT ONLY,
ROSSINI
Will start from Kapp Brothers, Tobacconists, Stephen's Green
On his 20-feet stilts, and race

THE TRAM-RACING STILT WALKER

The Tramcar to the Circus for a wager of £20
Starting at 7 o'clock precisely[1]

Rossini was a clown with the renowned Ginnett's Circus and before arriving in Dublin, they had played to packed audiences in Belfast. On many nights, there had not even been standing room. The circus was particularly well known for its leaping dogs and its horse show, interspersed with juggling and acrobatics. Touring with the company was a famous American rider, Louise Madigan, and crowds were thrilled by the high wire and clowns.[2] Victorian circuses differed from those of today in several ways, such as in the staging of competitions; these were not dissimilar to the contests that feature in modern American rodeo shows. Ginnett's Circus starred James Madigan, a champion pole vaulter, who double-somersaulted over elephants and horses. The elephants were also trained to perform in various other parts of the show.[3] In fact, the circus was so well known that it had entered popular Dublin parlance, invoked whenever there was a fuss of some kind. For instance, in *The Forest Fire and Other Stories* (1919), a character called Casey says, 'Shure there's hell an' all goin' on in Grafton Street … the way ye'd think Ginnett's Circus was comin' into the town.'[4]

In Dublin, Ginnett's set up home on the skating rink at Earlsfort Terrace, just off St Stephen's Green, where a temporary wooden hippodrome was built, including reserved areas and galleries around the viewing ring. News soon circulated about Rossini's extraordinary contest, and that evening hundreds of people gathered excitedly outside Kapp's tobacco shop on Grafton Street to see the challenger. Rossini did not disappoint, and at exactly seven o'clock he appeared in an upstairs window of the shop. To gasps from the crowd, he stepped out onto a long pair of stilts, at least twenty feet tall, and strapped them on. While he waited for the tram to arrive, he made a practice run. Under the watchful gaze of several police constables and the cheering crowds, he raced onto South King Street, William Street and Wicklow Street before returning to Grafton Street and onto St Stephen's Green.[5]

Now the contest between the stilt walker and the tram could begin in earnest. Rossini spotted a tram on its way to Rathmines. He took off at a quick pace and soon left the vehicle behind. However, just opposite the Royal College of Surgeons, disaster struck. Rossini had been accompanied all the way by a 'coloured gentleman' on horseback, but the animal suddenly spooked and hit one of the stilts. The acrobat was thrown to the ground with great force and all was silent. A crowd grew around him. Many thought he had died.

Then, amid great cheers, Rossini stood up and brushed himself off. Climbing onto an outside car, he told the people with a flourish: 'I am not seriously hurt. I have only got a shock, and I hope you will all attend the circus this evening.'[6]

The next day, the wife of the Lord Lieutenant, the Countess of Aberdeen, attended the three o'clock show at Ginnett's Circus with her family and attendants, escorted by a detachment of mounted DMP constabulary. The vestibule of the circus had been draped with curtains and the floor had crimson cloth laid

EXTRAORDINARY MATCH BETWEEN STILTS & TRAM-DUBLIN.

On his twenty-foot stilts, the redoubtable Rossini towered over
Dublin's trams. (*Illustrated Police News*, 26 March 1886)

on the floor. A private box had been opulently furnished by a
firm from Ormond Quay to receive the vice-regal party.[7]

During the show they watched Mademoiselle Mancini, a
bareback horsewoman, who performed to great applause. At a
quarter past four, the Lord Lieutenant, who had been detained
by business, arrived himself, accompanied by his private
secretary and aides-de-camp.

Before the circus left town, it was involved in a minor drama when the police caught a labourer trying to pawn some items of stolen clothing belonging to it. These included a coat owned by one of the circus grooms and the night watchman's suit, which the labourer had taken while he was cleaning the hippodrome. The DMP oversaw the city's pawn offices because stolen items often turned up in them. In this instance, the vigilance of Constable Hanley paid off and he was later praised for his efforts. For his part, the thief was sentenced to six months' imprisonment.[8]

Ginnett's Circus continued touring until the start of the First World War, when all its horses were confiscated for the war effort. Re-established in 1989, it is in existence today, although its acrobats no longer race trams on stilts.

13

THE BURGH
QUAY TRAGEDY

Evening in Dublin and the raucous cries of seagulls adds to a soundscape of clanging tram cars on O'Connell Bridge, the chug of Guinness boats plying their way on the River Liffey and trains coming and going from Westland Row Station. Near Hawkins Street, a young newspaper seller stands, crying 'Herald or Mail'. He stops in mid shout. Some corporation men had gone down a manhole into a sewer on the quays. It has been a long time now and they have not returned. The lad spots the silhouette of a tall policeman on the bridge. He runs for help.

Saturday was always a working day in Dublin. Workers finished early, but it was not part of their weekend. On 8 May 1905 Henry Martin, owner of a small firm contracted to Dublin Corporation, went down to the junction of Burgh Quay and Hawkins Street with three of his employees to work on one of the sewers. Their duty was to release water from the South Quay sewer into the main drain. The work went smoothly enough and, before leaving, Martin told the men to leave the sluice gates open for an hour. He then sent one of the men,

Christopher Breen, to the Pigeon House, where work was also being carried out.

That left the other two workers, John Fleming and John Coleman, behind. They waited as water continued to empty through the sluice gate. Fleming thought that a pipe below had burst, so he went down the manhole, but then he seemed to lose his balance and fall. Coleman went down to help, as did an engineer called Thomas Rochfort. They never came back up. Fleming was already dead.

When a sixteen-year-old newspaper seller saw that the men had not emerged from the manhole, he raced up the quays to O'Connell Bridge, where he found Constable Patrick Sheahan, 45B. The twenty-eight-year-old, Limerick-born constable had only come on duty to relieve a colleague so that he could go to the theatre. It was by a quirk of fate that he was out that evening.

Unmarried, Sheahan lived at College Street Station with his fellow officers.[1] He had already distinguished himself a number of times for bravery, and he was a popular officer on the force, having joined up eight years previously.[2]

In October 1902 he went to help rescue two families from a house that had suddenly collapsed on Townsend Street.

Constable Sheahan depicted in the *Irish Independent*, 8 May 1905.

The front wall was still standing, but inside, the rooms at the back were nothing more than a pile of rubble. Sheahan and the local fire brigade had to drill a hole into the brick wall outside and then get under the fallen part of the house. The rescue efforts went on until after dark, and eventually, by lamplight, the final inhabitant was dug out. Thanks to Sheahan's efforts and those of the fire brigade, all of the residents apart from an unfortunate old woman were saved.[3]

Two years later, in 1904 a large roan bullock escaped from its keeper while it was being driven along Harcourt Street near the train station. It ran off towards Wexford Street, where it knocked down a nine-year-old girl. From there, it headed for Whitefriar Street and struck a five-year-old boy, stumbling and rolling over on him. It got back to its feet, dashed along Stephen Street and finally emerged onto Grafton Street. By this time, it had left a trail of destruction in its wake. People scattered in all directions. It was followed into Anne's Lane by constables Sheahan and Kerby, guided by a local stableman. Finding its way blocked by tall buildings, the bullock suddenly wheeled about and faced the three men. First it charged the stableman, who took shelter, slamming a half door into the animal's face. As the bullock began to batter the door, the stableman hastily secured a rope and threw it out to the policemen. They succeeded in getting the rope around its horns, and a struggle ensued for twenty minutes. With the help of some members of the public, the constables wrestled the exhausted animal to the ground, and it was eventually slaughtered by a butcher from Capel Street.[4]

Now, a year later, Constable Sheahan was called into action again and he lost no time. It must have been an impressive sight to see the six-foot-four constable running down the quay. He was joined by a cabbie he knew called Kieran Fitzpatrick, or Fitz. They looked down into the open manhole and a noxious smell pained their heads. Before going any further, Sheahan sent the newspaper boy off to College Green to telephone for an ambulance. Next, the cabbie volunteered to attempt a rescue. Cautiously he climbed down, but when he reached the last rung, he realised with a shock that the ladder stopped about six feet short of the sewer. He had no option but to jump the rest of the way. Turning around, he spotted the three men lying in a heap at the bottom, a foot of water flowing over their faces.

Fitz tied a rope around one of them, so that he could be hauled up, and then returned to the surface. At that stage, Sheahan took off his helmet, belt and tunic to help the cabbie. 'Fitz, mind yourself!' Sheahan said. 'Go down the ladder.' The constable and the cabbie then descended into the darkness. The cabbie later told the inquest that, standing in the sewer, he

As the Burgh Quay tragedy unfolded, crowd control was a problem for the DMP. (*Weekly Irish Times*, 13 May 1905)

suddenly felt dizzy, as though he were in a dream, and he had a vague sensation of rain falling on him.[5] He blacked out.

By now a large crowd had gathered on the quay. Nobody knew what had happened to Fitz and Constable Sheahan; both were now unconscious. By the time the fire brigade arrived, the noxious fumes were starting to become unbearable at street level. One of the officers, Charles Mier, was lowered down on a lifeline with a lighted candle. Shortly afterwards he cried out to those on the surface, and ropes were thrown down, which he managed to get around three of the unconscious men. Another officer then went down. Eventually all the sewer workers, as well as Fitz the cabbie, were brought back to the surface, amid cheers. However, the police had to resort to violence to hold the crowd back, and one man was knocked to the ground. In the melee, his leg was broken. *The Irish Times* of 13 May 1905 described the 'pitiable sight' as the senseless bodies of the Corporation workers were laid out on the cobblestones, 'covered with the foetid slime of the drain … whilst their countenances were covered with blood, evidently caused by the men's falling and knocking against the side of the manhole.'

Meanwhile, a fireman named Lambert was still underground trying to rescue Constable Sheahan. Lambert was brought to the surface unconscious by a fellow fireman, but he was successfully revived and driven to Jervis Street Hospital. The crowd was now much larger, and people craned their necks to see what was going on. In an effort to keep the entrance to the manhole clear, the police struggled to keep them back, but there were not enough officers on hand. Watching the crush of bodies and realising the potential for further disaster, a journalist telephoned Dublin Castle, and within ten minutes forty extra constables, in the charge of an Inspector Grant, arrived.[6]

A labourer named John Murphy then stepped forward. He volunteered to go into the sewer for another attempt to save Sheahan. He disappeared down the manhole. After a few moments there was a tug on his line, and a moment later the tall, sixteen-stone body of the constable emerged from the sewer, feet first. He had now been down there for about half an hour. He was carefully laid on a stretcher, but onlookers could see that his lips were blue and his cheeks pale. He was beyond saving. A thrill of horror rippled through the crowd as his body was hoisted into an ambulance.

That was not the end of the ordeal, however. Just as the authorities prepared to close the manhole cover, somebody cried out that there was still another man below. Confusion reigned. Nobody seemed to know just how many men had gone down into the sewer. Another labourer, named O'Hara, went down to check, but when he didn't come back up three more men went down to rescue him, but failed. They were brought out, but now O'Hara was missing. Three firemen made unsuccessful attempts to rescue him and were brought back up. At the eleventh hour, a fireman called Kelly decided to go down again, this time with a smoke helmet. Groping in the dark sewer, he felt a man's cap in about twelve inches of water and then located the body of O'Hara who was still alive. Both men were brought back to the surface, and the manhole cover was finally closed.

This drawing captures the size of the crowd on Burgh Quay as the disaster unfolded. (*Irish Independent*, 8 May 1905)

On 15 May 1905 an inquest was held to investigate the deaths of Sheahan and Fleming. Sheahan's brother, John, was present. He was seven years the constable's senior and worked as a constable himself in A division in Inchicore.[7] Fleming was represented by his son, who told the jury that his father had left nine children behind, the youngest of whom was just fourteen months old. Dublin Corporation was represented by a law agent named Ignatius Rice, who was quick to absolve his employer from all responsibility on the basis that the sewer had not yet been handed over by the contractor, Mr Martin.[8]

The jury quickly reached the verdict that the constable had been 'rendered unconscious by sewer gas; sulphuretted hydrogen' and that he had 'suffocated in the liquid which was at the bottom of the main sewer by Burgh Quay'. With respect to the death of forty-two-year-old John Fleming, they remarked that this was an incident in which Sheahan had 'so gallantly lost his life'.[9] Nobody seemed to pay attention to Fitzpatrick, the cabbie, when he quite reasonably argued that 'whoever was in charge of the main drainage should be ashamed of themselves, as the ladder … did not go down to the bottom'.[10]

One overlooked aspect of this tragic incident is that just a year earlier, there had been a similar accident on Eden Quay. It also happened on a Saturday when four men working for Dublin Corporation were inspecting the main drainage works. Fortunately, on that occasion the men had been warned about the release of poisonous sewer gas, but even still one of them was brought up unconscious and the others 'were reeling about in a dazed condition'.[11] They were lucky to escape with their lives.

In the months after the Burgh Quay incident, the sewer rescuers were presented with medals of the Ancient Order of St John of Jerusalem by the Lord Lieutenant. This was followed by another award ceremony at the Mansion House, where Constable Sheahan was presented posthumously with a medal for bravery in the Oak Room. His brother was there to collect it. The lord mayor was sorry, however, that 'the plucky little newsboy who gave the alarm to the police constable was not amongst those honoured'.[12]

14

RABID DOGS

Anna Maria Collins writhes in agony in her hospital bed, straining violently against the straps that hold her down. Just a few days earlier her pet dog, a terrier, bit her on the lip. Now she asks to be allowed to die and not to be smothered. Wide-eyed, she refuses all water that is offered to her.

Dubliners were terrified of rabies, a disease that caused its victims to react with great fury. It afflicted them with restlessness, irritability, headaches and fevers. The brain swelled, followed by muscle spasms, vomiting, coma and death. When Ms Collins, aged twenty-five, contracted the disease – then known more commonly as hydrophobia – in July 1879, *The Freeman's Journal* reported it as a 'shocking case', and her fears about being smothered were not unfounded.[1] In May 1861, a young woman with rabies from Newport, County Tipperary, was smothered between two feather beds.[2]

When a dog was bitten and infected, the disease took up to two weeks to develop. At first the animal was inclined to keep to itself in some dark place and would refuse all food. Unlike an affected human, however, it did not always have a dread of water. After a time it would become lively again, running about mischievously and tearing and eating things, but it would not be able to resist snapping at passing objects, and as the disease started to advance, it would become more and more excited, with wild-looking, dilated pupils. A painfully swollen throat meant that it produced a strange, hoarse bark, and it would start to froth at the mouth. In what was known as 'dumb rabies', the lower jaw would fall slackly due to a swollen tongue, and the animal would tear at its jaws with its front paws. In the last stage of the disease, the dog would lose all recognition of its owner and, if let loose, fly onto the streets and bite everything it came across. Before Ms Collins's dog bit her, it reportedly went on a 'rabiferous' journey through the streets of Dublin.

In July 1844 a police order was passed directing officers to 'destroy dogs, or other animals reasonably suspected to be in a rabid state, or which shall have been bitten by any dog or animal reasonably suspected to be rabid'. This was followed by a proclamation from the lord mayor of Dublin requiring that all dog owners put muzzles on them or blocks of wood on their necks.[3]

On Sunday 28 August 1898 a man told the police at Newmarket Station that a black-and-tan collie, frothing at the mouth, had bitten a boy in Pimlico. Sergeant McDermott and Constable O'Meara of A division armed themselves with revolvers and went in search of it. Unknown to them, Constable O'Connor, 120A, had already come across the dog in Pimlico. He had succeeded in hitting it with his truncheon, the only weapon he had to hand, but the dog had escaped. On 30 August 1898 *The Freeman's Journal* reported that Constable

O'Meara had cornered a rabid dog in a yard at the rear of Meath Place. He fired at it, but the first bullet failed to kill it. The animal only succumbed after it was shot four times.[4]

One of the worst incidents by far occurred on 7 June 1885, when scores of people were bitten in Dublin as a result of two separate canine rampages. At eleven o'clock, while many people were at Sunday mass, a 'rabid brute' ran up from the second lock on the Grand Canal with two policemen, Sergeant Dunphy, 51A, and Constable Shield, 124A, following close behind on a car. As the dog raced down Echlin Street, the two policemen gesticulated wildly and aimed at the dog with their truncheons. From there, the car hurtled onto James's Street and Thomas Street, still chasing the dog. The animal bit seven people and eventually, having reached Meath Street close to Crostick Alley, it seized a little boy named Jason Shiel and began to worry him like a sheep. The two policemen 'succeeded in battering his skull with their truncheons'.[5] In all, eighteen people had been bitten, several of whom required treatment at Dr Steeven's Hospital and at the Meath Hospital.

Meanwhile, on the northside of the city, a large, rabid bull terrier appeared on Mountjoy Street. There were crowds of people out and the dog bit everyone it passed. These included Francis Fagan from Bessborough Cottages, who was bitten on both legs and had to be taken to the nearby Mater Hospital. The dog, meanwhile, reached Paradise Place, where it worried a goat to death. Passing through North Frederick Street, it attacked a young man called William Rooney and bit him on the face and right leg. From there it ran along Dominick

Street, Bolton Street and Capel Street, where it bit William White from Brush Row, Ormond Market, in two places on the left leg. Eventually it was shot by Constable John Brereton, 226D, in a house on Jervis Street.[6]

Rabies was not confined to dogs. In fact, it was more common in cows. On 1 August 1894 a mad cow rushed out of Francis Street into Dame Street. People scattered to take cover, some of them in nearby houses, while others tried to stop the animal. The cow injured several people, including one man who was knocked under a hackney car. She was eventually driven into a yard in Temple Lane, where Constable 174B shot her dead.[7]

During this period, when fear of rabies was at its height, there were regular articles in newspapers and magazines about the problem. For instance the *Irish Fireside*, which sold on the streets for a penny, included an article in its summer edition of 1885 entitled 'Mad Dogs! How to know them and what to do if bitten by them'.[8] The main method of treatment for rabies bites in Dublin hospitals was to cauterise, and thereby inflame, the wound. There was a belief that inflammation would prevent absorption of the disease into the bloodstream, and various caustic chemicals were used to make that happen. These included strong acids such as nitric and sulphuric, and salts such as sulphate of chloride. Zinc was also used, but if none of these were available, the simplest remedy was a red-hot poker or boiling hot water applied to the skin. As a last resort, the affected flesh could be cut out completely by a surgeon and the blood allowed to run, carrying away (so it was believed) the infection. Prior to attending hospital, Dubliners were advised by Dr James McKenny to pick up a stone on the street and 'bruise the part with a few severe blows of a stone' or even try to suck out the wound.[9]

Although rabies had been largely brought under control by the early twentieth century, there were still occasional incidents in Dublin from time to time. On 23 August 1913 Constable Johnson, 42B, acting on a tip-off he had received from a guest at the Shelbourne Hotel, went to a shop on Dawson Street. There he found a brown, rabid mongrel; he arranged for it to be taken to Lad Lane Station and had it shot.[10] In each such case, the veterinary department needed to check the carcass of the animal afterwards to verify the cause of death.

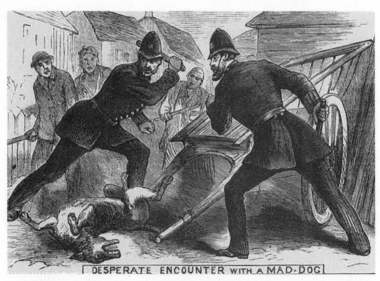

DESPERATE ENCOUNTER WITH A MAD·DOG

Dubliners lived in fear of rabid dogs. Once cornered, they were bludgeoned or shot by the police. (*Illustrated Police News*, 17 July 1886)

During a spate of rabies cases the police were directed to give special attention to unmuzzled or unlicensed dogs, but that had the effect of clogging up work at the police courts. Men rarely attended to answer the charge as they could not afford to lose a day's work; they sent their wives instead. In front of the magistrate, the owners often lied and said the animal was dead. These conversations could be quite confusing because when the clerk announced the summons, he called out the name of the dog owner, not the dog, to which the owner's wife would answer. It made it sound as though she had perpetrated a terrible crime: 'Call Peter Casey.' 'He's hung, sir; he was very owld and stupid, and hadn't a tooth in his head, so we hung him, not to be bothered with him anymore.'[11]

Frank Porter, who was a magistrate in Dublin during the late nineteenth century, recalled one particularly funny anecdote. A woman heard her husband, James Foley, being called, so she stood up and said:

'He's drownded, yer worship; we drownded him off Wood Quay, the very evening that we got the summons. He wasn't logged or muzzled, but he is dead now, and the policeman 'ill never see him again.'

'You are fined two and sixpence.'

'Oh! Yer worship; that's very hard, and he dead.'[12]

In one particularly gruesome case, a dog owner brought the animal's pelt into court to prove it had died. In another incident, a man named North had to pay a fine after his rabid dog, which was unlicensed and not muzzled, bit a pig on the nose in Smithfield Market. The dog subsequently recovered, but the pig was no longer as valuable. When the dog appeared at Capel Street Police Court with its owner, the animal was subdued, as if it knew it was in trouble. The case was settled by the police magistrate, who, having set a high fine of one guinea for the attack, remarked that 'the dog would be slow to treat himself to pigs' noses' in the future.[13]

15

A HOG IN ARMOUR: THE SHOOTING OF THOMAS TALBOT

Unsteady on his feet, a man in tweeds puts a shilling down heavily on the bar. The landlady glances up; some of the clientele mutter that he is the hated informer Talbot. He is a marked man; his days are numbered. No amount of success at skittles or backgammon can save him now.

On the afternoon of 12 July 1871, retired RIC Head Constable Thomas Talbot went to Morton's in Harry Street, Dublin, where he sat and drank for most of the day. At last orders he downed two half glasses of rum, paid the landlady a shilling and set out for home. To some, the forty-five-year-old seemed to possess:

A decidedly handsome, manly countenance, which was rendered particularly impressive by his lofty, towering bald head. His eye was peculiar, and, perhaps, his worst point, being rather sunken under a full brow, and, though quiet in its motion, was severely or kindly as he felt.[1]

This epithet was one of the only favourable ones that Talbot ever received. He was popularly reviled as the *agent provocateur* who helped to foil the 1867 Fenian rising, and dramatist Dion Boucicault used him as the archetype for informer Harvey Duff in his 1874 production *The Shaughran*. In 1894 P. J. Tynan, an author and an extreme nationalist, gave a detailed account of his life and death in *The Irish National Invincibles and Their Times*,[2] and over half a century later, he was still remembered in songs and stories, as well as in plays such as Roger McHugh's *Trial at Green Street Courthouse*.[3]

His notoriety was earned in part by the efforts he made to imprison Fenians, and in his speech from the dock against the journalist, Stephen Joseph Meany. Meany, who provided his own eloquent defence after he was accused of having made treasonous speeches against the Crown in New York, infamously described him as a 'hog in armour'.[4] As a result, several attempts were made on his life, one of which resulted in the shooting of an innocent man on Ormond Quay in late 1867.[5]

By the summer of 1871 there were concerns for Talbot's safety, and Dublin Castle's detective division warned him to keep a low profile. After leaving Morton's, he spoke to a couple of friends before parting company with them. He passed over Carlisle Bridge and down Sackville Street. The remainder of his route along the east side of Rutland Square to his home in Dorset Street was unremarkable, until he reached the corner of Hardwicke Street. There his attention was arrested by a shadowy figure who stepped out of a nearby laneway. Before he had time to react, the man opened fire, hitting him in the side of the head.[6] The force knocked him against the railings of a house, but he managed to give chase for a short while. Two constables who were patrolling near St George's Church were just in time to see a bare-footed individual running into Upper Temple Street, but he levelled a six-chambered French revolver at them, firing several times and injuring one of them in the thigh. Before he had time to shoot again, the second constable pinioned his arm and struck him on the forehead with his baton.[7]

The shooting of Thomas Talbot on Hardwicke Street.
(*Illustrated Police News*, 22 July 1871)

Meanwhile, Talbot was well enough to walk to Green Street Station, where Inspector Gorman did his best to staunch the bleeding from behind his left ear. Mindful of the dictate that 'in applications for admission as patients, members of the police force are to have a preference', he arranged for the injured man to be taken to the Richmond Hospital.[8] There, Dr Agmon Vesey, a senior resident pupil, administered stimulants and discovered that the wound was no bigger than 'a good-sized pea'. He had a ready supply of emergency medicines to hand, which included tartar emetic, stimulants and leeches, but lost no time in sending for two of the most eminent doctors in Dublin, Mr William Stokes Jr and Mr John Hamilton. On arrival, Stokes performed a probe and quickly deemed Talbot to be suffering from a gunshot wound over the temporal bone – the portion of the skull that lies behind the ears on either side of the head.

Unless a shooting injury was relatively uncomplicated, most surgeons adopted a conservative approach. Essentially this entailed the daily administration of opium, or its brandy-based tincture laudanum, but such remedies were often insufficient to fully analgise the sufferer's pain, and many patients – such as Michael Briscoe, who accidentally shot himself in the stomach in Gregg's Lane in February 1868 – failed to obtain any real relief.[9] Initially the Richmond doctors took a similarly guarded stance with regard to Talbot, and in the absence of a pathology laboratory, radiology department or modern theatre, their methods were necessarily palliative.

Today cranial surgery is normally only performed in gunshot cases when a cerebral haematoma has been identified on radiological imaging. In the absence of such advanced techniques, Dr Stokes had no way of telling whether any internal bleeding was present. He passed a silver probe (a needle-like instrument) into the track of the wound, but it was difficult to see in the flickering candlelight. Meanwhile, a group of policemen gathered outside, waiting to take a statement from the injured man.[10]

On the morning of 12 July, Talbot lay senseless on a Richmond Hospital operating table in front of a distinguished coterie of doctors who, for reasons known only to themselves, had decided to perform surgery. Was it for humanitarian reasons? Did they feel capable of saving him so that perhaps he might, in a manner similar to Dr Sturk in Sheridan Le Fanu's *House by the Churchyard* awake from his coma to dramatically name his assailants? Or was it out of some colder, more anatomical interest? Whatever the case, the room was situated directly above the morgue, a fact that the Board of Superintendents of the Dublin Hospitals did not fail to notice when they made their inspection in 1879. They reported the presence of several unhygienic and foul-smelling 'dairy yards in close proximity of the hospital walls' and later commented that 'it is obvious that this is a most unsatisfactory arrangement and that the success of surgical operations is greatly imperilled by being performed in such an atmosphere'.[11]

When it came to the pursuit of anatomical knowledge, doctors were not so concerned whether their subjects were living or dead, and prior to the introduction of the 1832 Anatomy Act, lectures on gunshot wounds often consisted of firing bullets into cadavers. Such instruction was commonplace in Paris, where the bodies of deceased indigents were often used.[12] In Dublin, the lectures were conducted by Dr John Timothy Kirby, a veteran surgeon of the Spanish Peninsular War. When the enigmatic 'Erinensis' (possibly Dr Peter Hennis Green, the *Lancet*'s Dublin correspondent) included him in his contemporary *Sketches*, he noted that he was wont to employ the services of the resurrectionists to supply corpses from Bully's Acre for his classes. He leaves us with the following account of a lecture he witnessed at the Theatre of Anatomy and School of Surgery in Peter Street:

> The 'subjects' being placed with military precision along the wall, the Lecturer entered with his pistol in his hand and levelling the mortiferous weapon at the enemy, magnanimously discharged several rounds, each followed by repeated bursts of applause. As soon as the smoke and approbation subsided, then came the tug of war. The wounds were examined, arteries were taken up, bullets were extracted, bones were set, and every spectator fancied himself on the field of battle, and looked upon Mr Kirby as a prodigy of genius and valour *for shooting dead men*.[13]

In time the passing of the 1832 act put paid to this practice, and by the 1860s the use of anatomical drawings and museums had surpassed the role of dissection in surgical teaching.[14]

While gunshot cases were occasionally treated in hospital theatres, this was not necessarily due to sanitary concerns but because they afforded better sources of illumination. When enough sunlight was available, the operation was liable to be conducted on the ward. Extraction demanded great care, and some writers, such as John Hunter, advised against it. For some time Dublin surgeons had observed the change from musket balls to long, coned bullets with dismay, since the conical end acted like a wedge, driving through tendons and other soft tissues that together might have slowed a more primitive projectile. It was a simple design innovation but one that entailed a more complex extraction. In particular it was of utmost importance to ensure that the long axis of the bullet was removed in line with the track of the wound. Otherwise, there was a risk that its tip might tear some internal structure on its way out and cause further complications.

In Talbot's case, Dr Stokes used a Nélaton probe, an instrument that was fast gaining popularity in gunshot cases. It consisted of a small knob of porcelain placed at the end of a slender metal stem, the purpose of which was to take an impression of a leaden bullet or rusty iron projectile when it was placed fairly and directly against it. In failing to find the bullet, Stokes readily admitted that the instrument was not infallible and could not work if the ordnance had sunk into a cleft of bone or if there was overlying skin or muscle. When he returned to the theatre later that same day, he was joined by a cast of Dublin's most respected surgeons, including Oscar Wilde's father, William, and a veteran of the Crimean War, Robert McDonnell. Later he recorded that:

What was done was simply to enlarge the wound, cutting with a small scalpel horizontally from before backwards. In doing this, two arteries were severed: one was a very small vessel, which was at once secured by a ligature; the other was a larger one, and was either the occipital artery, or a large muscular branch ... there was no strong jet of blood from it; but it was obvious that a considerable vessel had been divided, from the rapid manner in which the wound filled up with blood. After sponging out the wound, Mr Hamilton made pressure with the index finger of his right hand against the temporal bone, and in this way haemorrhage was promptly arrested.[15]

As part of his post-operative technique, the surgeon usually inserted a digit into the wound and roved it around gently to ensure that a piece of cloth had not lodged there. The method was practised by many surgeons prior to Joseph Lister's discovery of antiseptic techniques, including Thomas Longmore, who wrote a number of American treatises on gunshot injuries. He described the finger as perhaps the most effective implement at the surgeon's disposal.

Talbot was not doing too well, either before or during his surgery. The doctors had failed to retrieve the bullet, and after he returned to the ward he began to exhibit some alarming symptoms, such as clammy perspiration, a tremulous tongue and fixation and retraction of the head. On 13 July Dr Stokes ordered 'draughts containing camphor and solution of muriate of morphia'.[16]

During their grand rounds, the Richmond surgeons watched carefully for signs of paralysis in their patient. This was a prudent approach, since they later discovered that Talbot's atlas, the first cervical bone of the spine where the spine meets the skull, had been fractured. In the case of suspected Fenian informer George Clarke, who was shot on the Royal Canal in February 1866, the paralysis of 'his lower limbs and left arm' described by Stapleton was almost certainly worsened by an overzealous policeman who put him into a sitting position on the towpath.[17]

By 15 July Talbot's pulse had become shallow and weak, and he insisted on having his brother telegraphed for. He subsequently became delirious, and it took the strength of several orderlies to restrain him. With dismay, Dr Stokes wrote:

> His pupils began to dilate, then to contract, and then to dilate enormously again. The respiration became stertorous, then 'blowing', and subsequently diaphragmatic. The violence of his struggles surpassed anything I have ever seen even in cases of the most violent delirium; and his screams were very loud.[18]

According to the proprietor of the *Irishman*, Richard Pigott, he called an attendant in one of his more lucid moments to ask:

> 'When will the doctor come?'
> 'At two o'clock,' was the reply.
> 'I'll be in hell then,' said the wretched man.[19]

Talbot was seen again at three o'clock on 16 July by surgeons

Stokes, Adams, Hamilton, Wilde and Porter, but he slipped into a coma shortly afterwards and died.

The inquiry into Talbot's death, held at Richmond Hospital, was limited to his skull vault, brain and atlas. Afterwards the governors deemed it prudent to bury his body in a secret plot. In the aftermath of the 1867 rising, the police superintendent of A division had written to the governors of the Meath Hospital advising them to arrange internment of another alleged informer's corpse as soon as his inquest had ended, to avoid a demonstration.[20] There were similar fears about Talbot's burial.[21]

In the months that followed, preparations got underway for the trial of Robert Kelly – the man whom the police had arrested on the night of 12 July under the pseudonym of Pemberton, the name by which he hoped to evade the clutches of the law. Funds were raised for his defence as far afield as Liverpool and Lancashire, and when the trial began large crowds of people came out to cheer him.[22] A banner was even draped over Pill Lane in Dublin with the legend 'God Save Kelly' written on it.[23] The case concerned the entire medical community because the prisoner's counsel, Isaac Butt MP, had prepared his defence on the basis that Talbot died from the surgery he had received at the Richmond Hospital. Aside from his record of defending Fenian prisoners, Butt was also leader of the Home Government Association – an organisation that championed the idea of limited autonomy for Ireland through a system of federal government with the United Kingdom. With a laconic twist, he suggested that instead of his client being put on trial for murder, it ought to be Dr Stokes who should be tried for Talbot's manslaughter.

Butt described Talbot's surgery as nothing more than an attempt to 'hack and mangle' him and claimed that Stokes was guilty of grinding his bones 'to dust' in the process.[24] During the trial, a portion of the base of Talbot's skull was produced (the suture where a piece of bullet lead was embedded between his occipital and temporal bones) as well as his atlas (the first bone of his spinal column).[25] One can only imagine the reaction of his brother, who appeared in court as a witness for the prosecution. For the surgeons, however, the presentation of such anatomical evidence was already becoming controversial, even though the damaged bones of gunshot victims were deemed to hold instructional value and, after the passing of the Anatomy Act, were considered vital for surgical instruction in Ireland.[26]

Ultimately, the prosecution claimed that Talbot's brain inflammation had caused his death, but when the defence team asked a medical student to produce the original set of notes, he came back from the hospital empty-handed and had to be sent back a second time, when he had more success. It quickly became apparent that the version supplied to the court was a sanitised adaptation of the original, designed to deflect liability away from the Richmond Hospital surgeons. Astonishingly, the real notes appeared to support Butt's claim that Talbot had died as a result of haemorrhage brought on by the operation. In his examination of the case in 1946, Irish lawyer and writer, Terence De Vere White, concluded that 'Dr Stokes' evidence at the inquest had afterwards been developed to produce a diagnosis of inflammation of the brain and the notes of the medical student adapted to suit such a theory'.[27] Robert Kelly was duly acquitted but subsequently convicted to twenty years' penal servitude for shooting another policeman, Constable Mullen.

The shooting of Thomas Talbot was merely part of a wider problem for the DMP during the late 1860s and early 1870s. Robert Kelly was a member of a Fenian assassination circle that had been active in Dublin since around 1865 and the police were afraid that his compatriots would attempt to free him during the trial.[28]

Aside from murdering informers and threatening those who sought to leave the Irish Republican Brotherhood (IRB), the gang watched the movements of certain policemen and high-ranking officials. Among their targets were Superintendent Daniel Ryan, who was head of the detective division at Dublin Castle, and Acting Inspector Edward Hughes. Hughes, who was shot with Acting Inspector Doyle in November 1865 as he made his way into the detective offices, had actually dis-covered, courtesy of an informer, that 'in New York, it was commonly declared that Hughes and Ryan ... ought not be allowed to live'.[29] Fortunately, he and Doyle were shot at from a good distance away and they sustained little but bruises, the bullets lacking the power to even tear their clothes.

Thereafter, the assassination circle shot several DMP con-stables in 1866 and 1867, as well as some civilians. These inclu-ded an attack on a commercial agent named Robert Atkinson on Ormond Quay in a case of mistaken identity. According to the undersecretary at Dublin Castle, Inspector Talbot was known to make his habitual homeward journey along the quays from the Phoenix Park and with their plan formed; the men lay in wait:

> A man was seen approaching. Walsh at once pointed him out as Talbot. Lennon [leader of the assassination circle] then put the others back, went up and fired two or three shots at this man who turned out to be a Mr Robert Atkinson, a tobacconist. The assailants seemed to perceive their mistake and decamped ... Mr Atkinson was badly wounded in the neck but he failed to identify any of the parties and accordingly all escaped punishment.[30]

Atkinson had a sword cane, but he was shot before he had a chance to use it.[31]

For a time, the threat to the police was so great that they were temporarily armed with firearms and cutlasses, and they went into some parts of the city in pairs. Dublin could certainly be a dangerous place; the lot of a policeman was not always a happy one.

16

A CASUALTY OF DUBLIN'S DYNAMITE WAR

Christmas Eve, 1892. With a deafening roar, all the windows on the side of City Hall and Exchange Court, the offices of the detective branch of the DMP, are blown in. Outside, on Dame Street, a man walking along the tram track reels with the force of the concussion and a passing lady is thrown into hysterics. The glass in several buildings, including Behan's public house, are shattered, and neighbouring householders watch as their crockery rattles on the shelves. A great many birds belonging to a naturalist named Madame Margotte, whose No. 1 Dame Street shop is on the very corner of Exchange Court, are thrown to the ground, and a large aquarium smashes, spilling goldfish onto the floor. The night is sharp and clear. With a wind blowing from the southeast, the boom can be heard up to five miles to the north and west of Dublin.

Several hours earlier, the atmosphere at Exchange Court, the blind alley off Dame Street that housed the detective division, had been festive. The mood at nearby Dublin Castle was optimistic. It was hoped that the prime minister, William Gladstone, might support national aspirations with the passage of his second Home Rule Bill, and for some at least the future looked bright. From an early hour on Christmas Eve the streets of Dublin were alive with people. Braving squally wind and rain, they jostled shoulders on both sides of the Liffey buying up holly and ivy, Christmas fruits, cakes, greeting cards and sweetmeats. *Sinbad the Sailor* was due to start at the Gaiety Theatre and, on the northside of the city, Mexican Joe's Wild West Show was going from strength to strength.

There were a number of men at the detective office that evening. Six were asleep upstairs, but a noisy group of eight congregated in the mess room. It was festooned with evergreens and Japanese lanterns in anticipation of the annual Christmas Eve dinner.

At eight o'clock that evening, Detective Constable Patrick Sinnott passed the electric lamp on Cork Hill and into the gas-lit court to report for duty. The twenty-nine-year-old Carlow man had served for four years as a DMP constable. He had been appointed to G division as an ordinary constable in 1889 and was now serving a probationary period as inspector. Three weeks earlier, he had suffered an attack of rheumatism of the knee, for which he had sought advice at the Meath Hospital. He was now returning to the married men's quarters with a ticket from the medical officer to say he was fit to work. During his absence, he had begun to grow a beard, which would undoubtedly afford him some protection from the cold winter weather.

At nine o'clock, Sinnott was dismissed with the other men with instructions to resume duty the following day from 4 p.m. to 6 p.m. He had two hours to spare before having to turn in to barracks for roll call. At a quarter to eleven he left the men and walked up to the corner of Dame Street. There he met James Clancy, caretaker of City Hall, and asked him to join him for a drink in Behan's across the street. They were joined by a Fenian named John 'Jackie' Nolan, and together they spoke happily about the forthcoming Leopardstown Races. Sinnott had a couple of half glasses of whiskey, and they left fifteen minutes later, just as the shutters were being put up. Several young lads had congregated around the mouth of the court and were bidding each other a merry Christmas. Outside, Dame Street was thronged with merrymakers walking in the direction of Christ Church to hear the traditional Christmas bells. Some played melodeons and concertinas.[1]

Sinnott wished Clancy good night, and the caretaker returned to his lodgings, where his newborn baby was asleep just under a window that looked onto the court. As Sinnott walked back to the mess hall, he noticed a small light glowing under the gas lamps on the pavement. A few moments earlier, Detective Constable Alfred Green had noticed the same object, but, thinking it might be the end of a smoked-out cigar, he had decided to leave it. Inspectors Dawson and Stratford had also passed by but noticed nothing, perhaps too deep in conversation.

Left alone on the quiet court, Sinnott was slightly more inquisitive. Perhaps his previous training as a schoolteacher had imbued him with a sense of curiosity. On closer inspection, the light appeared to be connected to a brown paper parcel. Whatever it was, it was small – about the size of a packet that might carry a bun or a copy of the New Testament. It had a very irregular shape. He bent down to take a closer look. At that moment, the clock at Christ Church Cathedral struck eleven.

Inside the detective office the door leading from the yard was thrown violently back, slamming Detective Constable Sloane into the wall and driving small fragments of glass into his face. The centre window was completely blown in, along with the shutter, and the iron bolts that held it fast shot with terrific speed across the room into the opposite wall, striking and loosening a board for hat and coat pegs. An Inspector Montgomery, who was on his way to write a report, was left reeling from the blast. In his own words, he felt like 'a man who had made a header into deep water and had come up gasping

Sinnott attempts to pick up the bomb. (*Illustrated Police News*, 7 January 1893)

for breath. My lungs felt compressed and for a moment I could not breathe.'[2] Upstairs, a sleeping detective was thrown out of his bed.

The shock of the explosion was so great that for a few moments those who stood on Dame Street or in the adjacent detective office were stunned. A man was knocked out of the seat of his horse-drawn trap and a boy received head wounds from flying shrapnel. There were a few moments of silence, punctuated by a low, ominous rumble. Glass continued to fall slowly onto the street like rain.

Inspector Dawson emerged first through the kitchen, joined by some other officers, but the caretaker's wife, whose baby was miraculously unhurt, would not allow her husband to go back outside. Inside her shop, Madame Margotte lay stunned under a shower of glass. Somewhere above her, a macaw began to squawk, 'O mamma, what is the matter?'[3] Within a few minutes, the street outside Exchange Court began to fill with curious onlookers. Pushing past them, Inspector George Flower from College Street division and a Superintendent Laracey arrived on the scene from the Lower Castle Yard.

Dr Alexander Smith came running from his surgery in nearby Parliament Street. Through a blueish, gunpowdery smoke, he found the mutilated figure of a man lying on the pavement, covered by dust and debris and surrounded by a civilian and two policemen named Hynes and Long. At first they thought that Constable Sinnott might be the dynamitard, his face having been disfigured beyond all recognition. His beard had been almost burned off his chin, but that was the least of it. His right hand and a portion of his arm were missing, and his right leg, the boot from which had been blown off, now clung to his body by a scrap of flesh. Horrifyingly, he was still alive.

Dr Smith commandeered a passing jarvey car, instructing two officers from B division and a passer-by named Samuel Reeves to lift the injured man onto it. As they did so, a trickle of blood ran from Sinnott's right leg onto the doctor's arm. He instructed the driver to go to his clinic, since the journey to Jervis Street Hospital might prove too much for the hapless constable. During the short ride, Reeves supported Sinnott's lower limbs while the two policemen supported the upper part of his body.

At the Parliament Street surgery Smith, joined by his assistant Mr Palmer, laid the body on a mat and made a careful examination. At first glance it reminded him of a corpse he had once studied after a blasting accident. He discovered that Sinnott's leg was broken at the lower third and that it was attached only by the calf muscles. Dr Smith carried out an amputation while Palmer applied a compress to the popliteal artery – the vessel immediately behind the knee. Samuel Reeves helped him to dress the stump with lint.[4]

Next, Smith examined the policeman's arm. He cut the sleeve from the shoulder down and discovered a bullet-like wound in the middle. Part of the forearm was protruding where the muscles had been torn away. Later he stated that:

The head was much singed, the eyelids blackened and swollen and his right ear was split at the rim. I sponged the face with cold water and gave him a stimulant which he swallowed. It apparently had some effect for he then began to moan.[5]

Since there might still have been a chance to save the young officer's life, Dr Smith sent to Jervis Street Hospital for a stretcher. While he waited, he received a visit from Police Commissioner David Harrel, Chief Superintendent John Mallon and Superintendent Laracy. Despite the injuries, they were able to identify the young man, and since no explanation of his condition was necessary, they left to seal off Exchange Court from the large throng of bystanders.

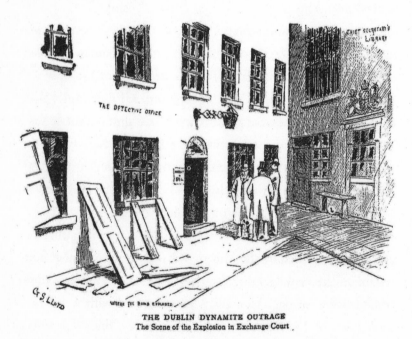

THE DUBLIN DYNAMITE OUTRAGE
The Scene of the Explosion in Exchange Court.

The damaged detective offices at Exchange Court, Dublin after the dynamite explosion. (*The Graphic*, 31 December 1892)

Meanwhile, Smith accompanied his wounded charge to the hospital. Samuel Reeves also insisted on staying with them. They arrived there shortly after half past eleven and were met by Dr Henry Grattan Day and Messrs McEvoy and Dalton, who helped to undress the policeman and put him to bed. By now Sinnott, his face black, torn and covered with blood, had lapsed into unconsciousness and could not be roused.

In the meantime, another messenger was sent to the High Street home of staff surgeon Dr Louis Byrne, who was on accident duty. Byrne was not at home, but somewhat fortuitously he had heard about the incident while he was in town and arrived at the hospital of his own accord. Losing no time, he commenced an examination, discovering, just as Dr Smith had done, that Sinnott had borne the brunt of the damage on his right side. His right arm and leg were almost amputated, with jagged, protruding bones. The surgeon ordered dressings to be applied as well as a dose of laudanum, but almost as soon as he was finished, the young policeman died. At the same moment the bells of Dublin's churches struck midnight, pealing out glad tidings – another Christmas Day had arrived.

The next day a number of visitors attended the scene of the explosion. These included the chief secretary, the attorney and solicitor generals, the lord mayor and a number of other notables. The view greeting them in the narrow court was one of utter devastation. The cobbles were covered with what *The Irish Times* of 27 December 1892 described as 'fine fragments of glass', and under the electric light they sparkled like a sea of diamonds. Over one hundred panes of glass in the detective office had been smashed, along with those on the City Hall side. Planks of wood had been placed over a gaping crack in the flags of the footway. The police officers on duty were under strict instructions to leave everything in position until the explosives expert arrived. One of Constable Sinnott's fingers had been found upstairs in the chief secretary's library.

The policeman was the first of several casualties during the Dublin Dynamite War – a series of bomb and arson attacks allegedly perpetrated by a small group within the IRB. The organisation vowed to achieve independence from Britain by violent means and during the early 1890s several other locations were targeted including Dublin Castle, the offices of the National Press, the Four Courts and Aldborough Barracks.

At daybreak on 28 December 1892 the young constable's remains were taken from Jervis Street Hospital and laid out in a coffin at the principal mess room at Exchange Court. From there, he was taken to the Lower Castle Yard and placed in an open hearse to be drawn by four black-plumed horses. His coffin was completely hidden under a blanket of wreaths sent by friends. On top a simple inscription read: 'Patrick Sinnott, aged 29 years, Died 24 December, in Jervis-street Hospital, R.I.P.'

As the members of the cortège lined up alongside the hearse, they assumed a rather spectral aspect – lent to them by the thick grey fog which had already blanketed the streets around the castle. At its head were the officers of B division, followed by the DMP brass band and a fife-and-drum band of the Gloucester Regiment, their instruments draped and drums muted for the occasion. This mingling of military and civil forces in mutual sympathy was, as *The Irish Times* of 29 December 1892 noted, 'an interesting and suggestive feature'. In other words, it was intended as a show of force against the IRB, a symbol of unity and solidarity in the face of extremist violence. Of note, the soldiers had themselves asked to be allowed to participate.

The hearse was protected by an honour guard of detectives, each with a black crêpe armband on his left arm, led by Sinnott's brother. The remainder of the cortège comprised a large body of police – five sergeants and a hundred men from various divisions, mounted and on foot, followed by inspectors and superintendents. Dublin Fire Brigade was also represented, led by their captain, Thomas Purcell, and bringing up the rear was the lord mayor's carriage and an open one containing the wreaths that could not be held in the hearse itself.

The cortège got underway at half past nine, leaving by the Cork Street gate. Outside, all the business premises were shuttered and silent. Despite the intense cold, large crowds stood and watched as the hearse made its slow way onto College Green, Westmoreland Street and across Carlisle Bridge, almost carving its way through the heavy fog. Reaching the top of Sackville Street, it continued up Rutland Square, the bands taking turns to play the 'Dead March' from *Saul*.

All through Phibsborough, the houses had their blinds drawn out of respect for the deceased man. When the hearse reached Prospect Road, the Gloucester Regiment struck up a touching piece of music entitled 'Farewell, My Comrade', switching to Chopin's 'Funeral March' when they reached the gates of Glasnevin Cemetery.

The funeral ceremony was held in the mortuary chapel, whose Dalkey granite did little to warm the attending mourners. The service was read by Reverend Father Coffey, and afterwards he joined the coffin as it made its last journey past the flanking yew trees towards the DMP plot at the rear of the old O'Connell Circle. There, on a headstone erected to the memories of those who had gone before, two names were picked out in red letters – those of constables John Cox and Joseph Daly. Both had died in violent circumstances. Sinnott would be the third such burial at the cemetery.

Later, *The Irish Times* commented on the huge outpouring of public sympathy for the young constable. Wreaths were laid by representatives of the Dublin pawnbrokers' assistants, the postmen of the Dame Street district and detectives from Belfast. The wreath left by Sinnott's own division simply read: 'In sad and loving memory of our departed comrade.'[6]

17

THE PHOENIX PARK DEER THAT FACED A COURT MARTIAL

A summer breeze blows gently through the grassy Hollow near Dublin Zoo. In the stand, the DMP band sits, dressed in their smart uniforms. Harmonies from brass and reed instruments mingle in the warm air, carrying the sweet notes of a waltz over the heads of ladies linking arms with moustachioed dandies, bare-footed street urchins from the tenements and the old fruit sellers who benefit from the passing trade.

The DMP band was a popular sight, and it performed concerts regularly in the Hollow at the Phoenix Park.[1] It was formed by Colonel Lake in August 1873, and it also often played in the Theatre Royal. In 1878 the Police Commissioner ordered that none of the men should wear facial hair, apart from moustaches, but he added that 'the bass drummer may wear all his beard if he chooses', presumably because he sat near the back and couldn't be seen.[2] The men went on parade drill every morning at 8 a.m. and if they had not shaved by the time that they fell in, they were liable to be reported.

The DMP band maintained a friendly rivalry with the RIC band, which it tried to outdo in terms of entertainment value. Once a year, for instance, the DMP band supported the Lifeboat Collection on Sackville Street. The boats were mounted on large wheeled frames drawn by teams of Clydesdale horses, and the various ship crews held out money bags on their oars for donations. As the band played, the city's fire brigade made the passers-by laugh by spraying them gently with water.[3]

The most amusing and touching story about the police bands of the time, however, is not about the DMP band but about Dublin's other Victorian police band, the famed RIC band, which was set up in 1861. It comprised twenty-five men in all, with a sergeant major, two sergeants, two corporals, two lance corporals and eighteen constables, and their uniform was of bright emerald green.[4] Just like their counterparts in the DMP, the men could be docked wages for playing poorly and there were some real stars within their ranks, such as J. Shelton, a cornet player who had the distinction of entertaining the royal family.[5] The men, who practiced at the police depot in the Phoenix Park, became extremely adept at drill manoeuvres, but when a large drum was presented to help them keep a marching beat, it had to be returned to stores because it was upsetting the nearby zoo animals.

During its history the band had several animal mascots and, arguably, this put them slightly ahead of their DMP rivals in terms of novelty. In 1915, for instance, a new bulldog was procured, and *The Irish Times* of 15 September hoped that he would 'cultivate a taste for music', unlike the previous dog, which had instead acquired a taste for several band members.[6] Two years later the bulldog was replaced by another mascot: an Irish wolfhound that proudly accompanied the band as it paraded through the streets of Dublin.[7] As a testament to the depth of feeling that the men had for these mascots, *The Irish Times* of 8 May 1920 reported the following:

> To the inexpressible regret of the Reserve at [the] Depot, the favourite band dog died on Friday (30th Ult). The dog was a comrade to all members of the Depot force, but had a decided antipathy to strangers. He was given a military funeral by the Fatigue Staff.

The tradition of the band mascot began during the late nineteenth century, when the bandmaster, concerned that the men were not playing their best, decided that they should have a lucky totem. Their first experiments in training a suitable candidate were not very successful – a cat ran away and a fox tried to rob a hen roost near the People's Gardens and had to be destroyed. Finally, a sergeant named Bartley managed to secure a young fawn from among the park's herd of free-roaming fallow deer.

The deer became quite tame – so tame, in fact, that it used to lie among the bandsmen during their practices wearing a collar and bells. The men named their mascot Phoenix, and understandably he was very popular among the ladies who visited the depot, as well as with the police commandant.

However, the good times were not to last. According to *Royal Irish Constabulary Magazine* of 1911:

He first gave overt evidence of ... inherent viciousness by nibbling at haversacks, eating up disciplinary files and destroying Depot passes. Pardoned for these pranks, in the next stage he took to the Phoenix Park, upset children, upturned perambulators, butted nurses and rammed every mortal unprotected by some musical instrument.

An unexpected visitor – a frightened deer, pursued by hounds, jumps through a window. (*Illustrated Police News*, 31 March 1877)

Phoenix had now become a liability, and he had to be punished for his misbehaviour. He was put into a pen for a time, but instead of calming him down, imprisonment only made him worse. He went into a fit and attacked the first ladies he saw upon his release. That was the final straw, and the reluctant band members had no choice but to hold a kind of court martial in one of the orderly rooms and sentence him to 'banishment'.

At night Phoenix was taken down the steep incline to the Furry Glen near Chapelizod and tied, blindfolded, to a tree. It had been arranged that the next day one of the park-keepers would release him so that he could return to the herd. The men hoped that, disorientated by his blindfold, he would not be able to find his way back to the depot.

However, when the men awoke to the usual bugle call, or 'Rouse', the next morning, before the final notes had ended Phoenix was there, standing at the front gate, 'just as though he had returned off an all-night pass'.[8] Half-heartedly the band members tried to drive him away, but when they opened the wicket gate to lead him off, he bounded back into the depot and upset some cooks who were on their way into the kitchens to prepare the morning coffee. He then rushed one particularly fat cook, who fell down heavily.

For this last misdemeanour a death sentence was passed. Poor Phoenix was no more.

18

POLICING A TROUBLED CITY

At the turn of the twentieth century Dublin's citizens were still relatively well disposed to the DMP, but after the 1913 lockout riots on Sackville Street the tide of public opinion began to change. Increasingly the police were viewed as an oppressive apparatus of the state, although admittedly they never earned the same level of public distrust as the semi-militarised RIC that patrolled the countryside.

In August 1913 approximately 20,000 workers were 'locked out' by 300 employers in the city because of their attempts to unionise. At that time a third of the city's population lived in slums, with high infant mortality and dire conditions, and a movement for unionisation was sweeping the city.

The basic daily diet was meagre to say the least. Typically it comprised little more than a breakfast and supper of tea and bread (usually with butter or dripping) and a dinner of cabbage and onions, with occasional herrings or bacon. The *Irish Worker* of 4 November 1911 outlined the typical diet of a tailor's family who lived in Dame Court: they had dry bread and tea for breakfast, and only one other meal – a dinner of dry bread, herrings and (on occasion) porridge. Every evening, 'pickaroonies' could be seen on Moore Street, going from stall to stall in search of leftover cabbage leaves, herbs or other food to fill a pot.

The lockout had an almost immediate effect on the city's food supply because of striking farm labourers in the hinterland of the city. When 300 men employed by P. J. Kettle at Kilmore Santry struck work in mid-August 1913, their employer attempted to get around the problem by employing non-union outsiders, otherwise known as 'black leg' labour, but when the first delivery van arrived in Green Street it was met by a representative of the Irish Transport and General Workers' Union (ITGWU), who forced him to return to Raheny with the loaded cart.[1] A few days later the police began to make arrests and a number of men were brought before the courts in an attempt to break the deadlock.

By September the trading situation in the city was quite bad. With no supplies coming in, the women stood with empty stalls or hovered around the corporation fruit and vegetable market, the central supply depot for nearby Moore Street, in the hope that they might be able to buy enough to fill a basket car. 'It is like Sunday along the quays,' *The Freeman's Journal* opined:

No labour is about, big lines of berths unoccupied by steamers, not a smoking funnel, save at the berths of the City of Dublin steam packet company; very few carts on the move, a strange quiet everywhere. The voices of women, the rattle of cranes, the whistling and shrieking of sirens all absent; warehouses overflowing with crates and packing cases on the North Wall so that carts can hardly get past the obstructive mountain ... the effect of the dispute in the suburbs is very distinct. People do not come into the city ... for obvious reasons. They are afraid of disturbances, and they cannot get home.[2]

The disappearance of so many tram and train commuters robbed local traders of yet another source of revenue. Most evenings, they were able to set up stalls outside theatres, music halls and picture palaces to sell fruit to the crowds, but now these venues lay eerily quiet.

Meanwhile, the ordinary rank-and-file members of the DMP who moved to break up strikes, raid houses and attack rioters were, for the most part, no better off than the rest of the city's workers. For instance, a labourer could expect to earn just over £1 a week during the summer when fully employed, but that was roughly equivalent to what a newly fledged policeman might expect to earn. Moreover, they were put into a difficult and compromising position, as they were often asked to treat their own neighbours with great harshness.[3] There was nothing new about these working conditions. As far back as 1891 James P. O'Byrne, editor of the *Constabulary Correspondent*, had said: 'I have reason to know that the Force is at present seething with discontent ... [the men are] holding arms against their own countrymen in their own land – constrained to uphold laws which have been repealed over and over again, because they were inimical to the same countrymen, and still, though

A RIOTOUS LIVING---D.M.P. AND SALARIES

The Officer of Peace---- And Plenty.

In response to a quip from a Dublin Disturbances Commission official about how lucky he is to receive presents, a constable shakes out a bag of glass bottles, abuse notes and bricks onto the table. (*Sunday Independent*, 1 February 1914)

hateful to their own minds, they have been obliged to carry out these laws in practice.'[4]

Dublin newspapers carried 'daily reports of court proceedings arising out of assaults on the police on duty', so it seems the DMP had reason to feel they were under siege.[5] With the advent of online newspaper archives, it is now quite easy to trace individual badge numbers and thereby get some insight into what working life was like for the DMP during this troubled period. What becomes apparent is that in some districts many of the officers were overworked. This was particularly evident among the officers of B division, who were once described by Fenian leader John Devoy as the 'grenadiers of the force' on account of their height and soldierly bearing.[6] In just three short years, for instance, Constable 37B dealt with cases of intimidation, stone-throwing at trams, rioting and looting, as well as all of the ordinary things officers on the beat were supposed to handle – cases of burglary and theft, domestic quarrels and public-house disputes.

One of the most infamous events involving the DMP occurred on 31 August 1913, later known as Bloody Sunday. It would serve to compound the misery that individual officers faced in terms of poor pay and conditions because, afterwards, they had to face public ire for their efforts to police what was, in effect, a very difficult and chaotic series of riots.

On 28 August Labour leader Jim Larkin was arrested and then released on bail. He announced that there would be a public demonstration on Sackville Street that Sunday, and he burned a proclamation issued by the chief magistrate prohibiting it. The assistant commissioner of the DMP, Sir David Harrel, convened a meeting with all his superintendents and told them to assemble a force of police on the street. There were to be five superintendents, nine inspectors, twenty-three sergeants and 274 constables, seventy-two of whom were from the RIC, drafted in to help the DMP deal with the unrest. The brief was quite simple: no assembly of workers was to be permitted and the police were told 'to advise persons to pass along, and not to remain about'.[7]

The previous evening there had already been violence in the city, first at Ringsend and then across the inner city as workers, angered that the tram drivers had failed to support their strike by continuing to operate a service, began to riot.

On Saturday, as Bohemians and Shelbourne met for a charity match inside Shelbourne's new football ground, the police moved to subdue a hostile crowd outside. The crowd was eager to disrupt the match because Larkin had told them there were scabs playing. The police dispersed the rioters with batons drawn, and during the melee one protester slipped a policeman's sword out of its scabbard and jammed it between the legs of a horse, felling the animal and its rider.[8] Violence also broke out elsewhere in the city. In Great Brunswick Street, a horse-drawn *Independent* newspaper van, protected by two policemen, was seized by a crowd, and Constable O'Callaghan, one of the escorts, was beaten and kicked on the ground.[9] Men who went to the assistance of the officers were also attacked, and when the police tried to make an arrest, their prisoner was freed by the crowd. A larger force of police then charged the crowd but was forced to retreat.

At Liberty Hall, rioters peppered the police with a fusillade of stones and bottles. Afterwards, as the crowd was driven onto Eden Quay, James Nolan, a thirty-three-year-old labourer from Spring Garden Street, North Strand, was fatally injured.[10] He was perhaps just caught up in the confusion. Robert Monteith, a British Army captain and workers' rights advocate, witnessed what happened:

He was walking quietly down Eden Quay when he was met by a mixed patrol of Dublin Metropolitan Police and the Royal Irish

Constabulary. The strength of the patrol was about thirty-five, all more or less drunk. One of the constabulary walked from the centre of the road on to the sidewalk and, without the slightest provocation, felled the poor man with a blow from his staff. The horrible crunching sound of the blow was clearly audible about fifty yards away. This drunken scoundrel was ably seconded by two of the Metropolitan Police, who, as the unfortunate man attempted to rise, beat him about the head until his skull was smashed in, in several places ... for saying 'You damn cowards'. I was instantly struck by two policemen and fell to the ground, where I had sense enough to lie until the patrol had passed.[11]

Later, Nolan's case was discussed in detail during a commission of inquiry set up to investigate the riots. The story was picked up by various newspapers that cited it repeatedly and it served to vilify the police, whose reputation suffered as a result.

The city was now like a powder keg that only needed a spark to set it alight. Realising how charged the atmosphere was in Dublin, some of the leaders of the ITGWU called off a rally they had planned for Sunday 31st. If their dictate had been observed, the events of Bloody Sunday may never have occurred. However, that same day, Jim Larkin, leader of the union, managed to sneak into the Imperial Hotel (now Cleary's department store) on O'Connell Street. He had made a reservation under the guise of a deaf clergyman named Donnelly, but when he arrived, he realised his room had flower boxes in the window. As he rushed to find a better vantage point from which to speak, he caught sight of himself in a mirror. He realised that his disguise, with a beard of grey hair and glasses to shorten his nose, looked 'too perfect', so he 'proceeded to tear out handfuls of the whiskers and threw them on the floor', to the amazement of hotel guests enjoying their coffee.[12]

Meanwhile, Countess Markievicz, whose husband, a labour sympathiser, had provided Larkin's disguise, drove to Nelson's Pillar with her friend, journalist and revolutionary Mrs Sidney Czira, on an outside horse-drawn car, and on arrival they found that a small crowd had already assembled. When the crowd recognised Markievicz, a cheer went up and the assembled people called for a speech. 'Move on,' said a DMP constable to the cab driver, 'or I'll have to take your badge.'[13]

As the party climbed down from the car, Larkin suddenly appeared at an upstairs window of the hotel and began to speak to the crowd. Immediately, the police rushed towards the hotel, seized Larkin and took him away. The countess took a slight blow from a baton and was cut. There was a surge from the crowd, and the police, thinking another riot was about to break out, began to attack them. Stephen Prendergast, a member of Na Fianna Éireann, a nationalist youth group, recalled:

Suddenly the cry was heard, 'a baton charge', and immediately there was utter confusion. The whole Street, or the people who were, unfortunately, traversing it, was set in motion. People ran hither and thither, the police on their heels chasing them. No time to ask questions, how or why this happened? I found myself, like other folk, running away from a group of policemen who were behind us wielding their batons. I made to get into one of the side streets and away from the excitement and, of course, the batons. But at every point that I tried to breach there was a sturdy posse of police in possession to drive us back into O'Connell St, and worst luck for some, into the line of fire of the police batons.[14]

As members of the DMP and RIC, some of whom were mounted, struck indiscriminately at men, women and children with their heavy truncheons, people fled in all directions but were followed into the side streets by constables who beat them to the ground. There are parallels to be drawn between what happened that day and the Sackville Street riots following the arrest of Charles Stewart Parnell, the leader of the Irish Parliamentary Party, in October 1881 when he told tenants to withhold rent from landlords. Ignoring the entreaty of Captain George Talbot to do their best to disperse the mob without batons, the police hid them up their sleeves 'so that a seemingly innocent bang with the forearm would become as momentous as the kick of a mule'.[15]

One witness to the Bloody Sunday violence was John T. Kelly (later known as Seán T. O'Kelly – future president of the Irish Republic). He was standing across the street near the General Post Office, where the situation was initially calmer, but was aghast when the police rushed across the road and kicked people 'in a shameful way'. Rioters fled from the baton-wielding constables into nearby Prince's Street beside the GPO, only to be caught between the constables and another party of police who were on duty at the rear of the *Independent* offices. Kelly and a gentleman tried to protect an old lady clutching a prayer book, but a constable told them, 'If

There were many parallels between the Sackville Street baton charge of 1881 and that of 1913. (*Illustrated London News*, 29 October 1881)

you don't get yourselves to hell out of that, I will let you see whether you will save her or not.'[16]

On the other side of the street, rioters mingled with people coming out of mass in St Mary's Pro-Cathedral on Marlborough Street, which added to the confusion. The riot lasted just minutes, but afterwards the scene on Sackville Street was one of great destruction; plate-glass windows had been smashed and tramcars were wrecked.

That night, the police went on the offensive and invaded nearby tenement houses, where they smashed furniture and wreaked havoc. In one such incident, a large number of constables and some members of the RIC were booed and stoned by a mob at the Gloucester Diamond. The police claimed they were provoked and were forced to rush No. 9 Gloucester Place because people were throwing stones at them from the windows; in one example, Constable 154C was struck by a 'jam mug' that was hurled from a top window. Sergeant 25C gave the order to rush the house, and the officers burst the front door in with their feet. They then made several arrests.[17]

In the aftermath of Bloody Sunday and the days surrounding it, a vice-regal commission of inquiry was established under the auspices of the Dublin Disturbances Commission to investigate whether the police had acted in a heavy-handed manner. In total, there had been fifteen riots in Dublin spanning four days. Five hundred DMP men had been mobilised (roughly half the total force) as well as 400 RIC officers hailing from many different parts of the country.

The sittings to investigate the conduct of the police during the riots lasted eighteen days and closed on 28 January 1914. Of the 281 witnesses called, 201 were members of the DMP. The verdict of the commission was that while some of the riots had been caused by police heavy-handedness, in general the DMP had carried out their duty patiently and with great courage, particularly as 200 members of the force had been injured.[18]

The riots in Dublin resulted in two highly publicised civilian deaths. After the Eden Quay assault, James Nolan's wife identified his body at Jervis Street Hospital. At the inquest, the members of the jury extended their sincere sympathies and accepted that his injuries had been caused 'by the blow of a baton' but added that 'the evidence is too conflicting to say by who[m] the blow was administered'. Similarly, in the case of John Byrne, a labourer who was found with a fractured skull at No. 4 Lower Gloucester Place, there was 'no evidence to show how [the] deceased received those injuries'.[19]

After the lockouts, there was further trouble ahead for the DMP. When the Easter Rising broke out in 1916, three police constables were shot and killed by the rebels. These were James O'Brien, who was shot in the head by an Irish Volunteer at Castle Gate, just off Dame Street; Michael Lahiff, shot on duty while at St Stephen's Green; and William Frith, shot in the head by a sniper who managed to fire through a bedroom window at Store Street Station. During the week of the Rising, a further six constables and a sergeant were injured.[20] Constable Cornelius Kiernan, one of the men who had arrested Jim Larkin in 1913, was lucky to escape injury when a bullet grazed him at Portobello as he was escorting a civilian to safety.

Because of incidents like these, the chief commissioner of the DMP ordered the withdrawal of the entire force from the streets shortly after hostilities broke out.[21] Within a short time, plate-glass windows had been smashed in the main thoroughfares and goods stolen. At the end of Easter week 1916, Irish parliamentarian John Dillon, who had been taking refuge in his home on North Great George's Street, wrote to his aunt, Lady Mathew. He informed her that:

A posse of about 10 policemen came down Gardiner's Row [*sic*] and passed on towards Findlater's Church – the first sight of a policeman's uniform I have had since Monday morning last. How strange the feeling of satisfaction and joy with which I saw the uniform as a sign of returning security and peace.[22]

Several members of the force were rewarded for their bravery during the Rising. These included Sergeant Patrick Haugh, who managed to rescue a police officer who had been seriously wounded; Constable Thomas Barrett, 67B, who arrested and disarmed a man threatening to shoot two soldiers; and Constable John Barton, 37B, who, during the first night of the rebellion, arrested at great personal risk a staggering twenty-seven looters in the vicinity of O'Connell Bridge. That same night, with the assistance of another officer, he arrested two armed men who were carrying a large quantity of ammunition. Another constable, James H. Coulter, 187A, was rewarded for conspicuous gallantry for his efforts to convey ammunition under fire to Dublin Castle and for 'disarming, after a severe struggle, a rebel who was attacking passers-by with [a] rifle and bayonet'.[23]

As daily life slowly returned to normal in the city, the police faced considerable difficulties trying to restore law and order. Their responsibilities included the retrieval of weapons, ammunition and explosives, as well as helping to ensure the burial of those who had died, when approached by a member of the public who had information about such unfortunates.[24]

One of the biggest challenges they faced was the arrest and

prosecution of looters, and the DMP prisoner book for the period 1916–18 is particularly revealing in that regard. From 4 May 1916 onwards, scores of cases are recorded, the majority of which relate to 'illegal possession'. Over the space of two days, seventy people were arrested, comprising an eclectic mix of street traders, factory girls, labourers and newspaper sellers. Their average age was just twenty-eight years old. They were charged at Store Street Station, and for the most part they hailed from Summerhill, 'Monto' and the tenements of Hardwicke Street. Among the more noteworthy entries are Michael Meleady, a thirteen-year-old schoolboy from Lower Gloucester Street, who was arrested for stealing two teapots. He claimed that another boy had given them to him, and he was merely cautioned and released. Richard Burgess, a newsboy from Cole's Lane, was not quite as lucky. He was sentenced to one month at St Kevin's Reformatory School for delinquent Roman Catholic boys in Glencree, County Wicklow.

Whereas the majority of those who were arrested had no jobs, William O'Keeffe, a tram driver from Mountjoy Parade, stands out in the book on account of him being in permanent employment. He was fined forty shillings.[25]

Many of the arrests were made after the police carried out house raids in the city. The *Daily Independent* of 11 May 1916 reported that looted goods had been concealed in local churches: 'Among the articles … in the Church of Our Lady of Lourdes, Gloucester St, were toys, tennis and cricket bats, rocking horses, cameras, jewellery, clocks, watches, rings, brooches, bracelets, mats, cloths and prayer books.'

Police stations in the city began to fill up with huge stockpiles of captured goods, including tonnes of flour and meal, sugar, tinned fruit and meats, soap, candles, salt and packets of starch, baking powder, cigars and cigarettes. Among the furniture items seized by the police were brand-new pianos, tables, chairs and dressing stands, as well as carpets and mats.

Despite a proclamation ordering people not to trespass onto Henry Street and other thoroughfares damaged by the fighting, the undersecretary at Dublin Castle noted that large crowds assembled regularly on Sackville, Henry and Mary streets.[26] A local shopkeeper named Kennedy wrote to inform him that as he was passing along Jervis Street, he was:

> Struck with a stone in the shinbone and another struck me on the side of the head. I will not say either was fired directly at me, as the firing was between two sets of youths, none of them over 18 years of age. It seems a deplorable state of affairs that since the Larkinite strike, this place has been left open to the rowdy element of this quarter. I would suggest the authorities to let the Corporation to have the place walled up (God knows it ought to be about time).[27]

It was very difficult to police what were now in effect open building sites filled with rubble. Nevertheless, Inspector John Mills from Store Street did not agree with Kennedy's claims. He defended the efforts that had been made to secure the area around the GPO, and he wrote that although large crowds of sightseers were indeed congregating in the area, 'disorder of the class described is not noticeable'.[28]

In the aftermath of the Rising, there was a short-lived attempt to arm the DMP. Rifles were issued to each of the twenty-four police stations in Dublin, and the men were trained in the use of these firearms.[29] A crowd of Dubliners gathered to watch as a force of fifty or sixty constables, equipped with their new, unfamiliar-looking weapons, paraded at Nelson's Pillar on O'Connell Street, *en route* to the military firing range at Dollymount Strand. Inevitably, they were jeered by the crowd: 'The brave soldiers! Bolting the stable, and the horse gone!'[30]

At Dollymount, the officers ate army rations in basic huts. They were instructed in weapons training by the RIC, but pay was a bone of contention. The men found the lack of a travel allowance to get to Dollymount every day particularly grating, and some took to cycling to the shooting range as a result.

During the summer of 1916 the policemen, pressing for better pay and conditions, began to hold meetings in the hall of the nationalist Ancient Order of Hibernians (AOH) on Parnell Square. The meetings were extremely well attended; upwards of 200 men took part. The city's newspapers did not report their resolution, passed on 20 July 1916, that if their demands were not met they would not be responsible for property in the city after 3 August.[31]

The government was led (mistakenly) to believe that the DMP was joining forces with the AOH. According to historian Gregory Allen, this misleading notion was encouraged by the AOH secretary, an MP named John Dillon Nugent. Predictably, the government worried that if the DMP took industrial action, the strikers would be issued with rifles from the police stations and the very men the government had armed to protect law and order might then take up arms against the state; in other words, they would have another rising on their hands. Within a short time, all the weapons were removed.

The dispute rumbled on, and charges of indiscipline were laid against a number of police constables on account of their continuing to attend meetings in the AOH hall, despite being warned not to. The truculent officers included Patrick Keating from Wicklow; James Daly from Cahirciveen, Kerry; Edward Smyth from Cavan; and James Murray from Dunmanway, Cork. Initially it was intended that the men would be dismissed from the force, but after an inquiry they were sent to various outlying DMP stations.

On 8 November 1916 a mock horse-drawn funeral was held in the city. A hearse, pulled by two horses, came to the C division headquarters in Store Street, where the station sergeant was informed: 'We're having a funeral.' The cortège then set off for A division, which took it across the River Liffey, watched by a bemused crowd of 'women and men of the working class'. Constable Smyth, one of the officers who had been punished by his superiors, climbed aboard at Kevin Street, and then the cortège, having picked up a hackney car, continued to Lad Lane, where it picked up James Murray. The cortège was now full of laughing policemen, and it refused to stop for an imposing seven-foot-tall traffic officer on College Green. The driver was 'a young constable dressed in the livery of a coachman'.[32] As a result of their prank, all the officers were dismissed from the force.

Overall, there is no doubt that the events of 1913 and the 1916 Rising took a toll on the morale of the DMP. The men clamoured for special treatment on account of the physical dangers as well as the public ire they faced in attempting to police the Irish capital. But their commanding officers were no less immune to criticism. On 27 July 1914 Sir John Ross, chief commissioner of the DMP, resigned, while his assistant commissioner, William Harrell, was suspended from duty by the chief secretary for adopting a heavy-handed approach towards the landing of rebel rifles at Howth prior to the 1916 Rising.[33] A career in the DMP was no longer seen as a job for life as it was now felt publicly that some measure of national independence would come and that the force would be disbanded. A time of change was now at hand.

19

IN THEIR OWN WORDS: FIRST-HAND ACCOUNTS OF POLICE WORK IN DUBLIN

William Richard Le Fanu

Born in 1816, William Richard Le Fanu was the younger brother of the famous novelist Joseph Sheridan Le Fanu. He was an accomplished man in his own right. He was educated at Trinity College Dublin, where he graduated with a Bachelor of Arts in 1839, and for much of his career he worked as a railway engineer. In 1863 he was appointed deputy chairman of the Board of Public Works. Prior to his death in 1894, his memoir, Seventy Years of Irish Life, *was published. The extract that follows, taken from that book, provides an interesting insight into police recruitment practices during the early days of the DMP.*

I had in that year [1839] become one of the pupils of Sir John

MacNeill, the well-known civil engineer. About a year after I had joined his staff I had gone to a fancy ball in the south of Ireland as an Irish peasant – frieze coat, corduroy knee-breeches, yellow waistcoat, grey stockings, and brogues; in my fist a good blackthorn, and on my head a wig, with the hair cropped quite close, except the national glib, or forelock, then the fashion amongst the southern peasantry.

When I came back to Dublin, I went to MacNeill's office dressed in the same way, and so perfect was the disguise that I completely took him in, as well as my fellow pupils. I told them I had come all the way from Clonmel to look for work, and couldn't find any, and wanted to get home again, but hadn't the means; and then and there they

Swearing in of special constables at Dublin Castle. (*Illustrated London News*, 9 September 1882)

made a subscription to enable me to get back to my native Tipperary.

Amongst the pupils was Hemans, son of Mrs Hemans the poetess, afterwards highly distinguished in his profession. He then lived in Dublin Castle, at the official residence of his uncle, Colonel Browne, Chief Commissioner of Police, with whom I often dined and spent my evenings. Hemans was so much pleased with the trick I had played that he insisted on my going to the Castle, disguised in the same way, to apply to his uncle for an appointment as constable in the Dublin Metropolitan Police, so I wrote a letter to Colonel Browne in my own name, saying that the bearer, Pat Ryan, was a most respectable young man, one of my father's parishioners, who was very anxious to be a policeman, and that I should be very much obliged if he could appoint him.

With this letter in my pocket, I took a covered car (there were no cabs in Dublin then), and drove to the police office in the Castle. I told the driver to wait for me, and was ushered by a policeman into a large hall where there were assembled several candidates for admission into the force, and also some constables. On entering, I looked about and said –

'Gentlemen, which of yez is Colonel Browne, if ye plaze?'

A policeman came up to me and said, 'Colonel Browne is not in the room. What is it you want?'

'Well, sir,' said I, 'it's a bit of a writin' that I have that Mr Le Fanu gave me for the Colonel.'

'Give it to me,' said he, 'and I'll give it to him.'

'Not by no manner of means,' said I, 'for Mr Le Fanu towld me not to give it to anyone, only into the Colonel's own hands; and, begorra, I'd be afeared to give it to anyone else, so I must see him myself.'

The policeman replied, 'If you don't give me the letter you won't see him at all. Don't be afraid. I'll give it to him safe enough.'

'Under them circumstances, sir,' said I, 'I'll trust you with it; but, my good man, you must give it to the Colonel at once, for Mr Le Fanu will be displeased if I'm kept waitin'.'

I was, however, kept a long time, during which I had a good deal of talk with the other candidates. Amongst them was a very dapper little fellow, neatly dressed, but plainly quite too small and slight for the police. He looked rather contemptuously at my get-up, and said – 'Now, do you think you have much chance of being appointed?' 'Well, my tight fellow,' said I, 'if we are to judge by personal appearance and shapes, I think I have as good a chance as you, anyway.' He retired and a friendly constable came up to me, and said, 'What part of the country do you come from?'

'I'm from Tipperary,' said I.

'I thought so,' said he; 'I partly guessed I knew the frieze. And in what part of Tipperary do you live?'

'Not very far from Newport,' said I.

'Oh, then,' said he, 'I suppose you know the Doodeys?'

'Of coorse I do,' said I. 'Why wouldn't I know them?' (I had never heard of them.)

'And how is old Mick Doodey?' said he.

'He's illigant,' said I.

'And how is Little Tom?' he asked.

'He's illigant too,' said I, 'only in regard of a sort of a swelling he has in his jaw.'

'He was always subject to that,' said he; then looking at my hair, which was too long, and was coming out below the wig at the back of my head, he said, 'What makes your hair so long at the back?'

'I suppose,' said I, 'when my hair was shaved off last Candlemas, when I had the sickness, that the front and the back of it grew longer since than the other parts.'

'Come in with me for a minute,' said he, 'and I'll crop it off for you in the way you'll look neat and tidy when you're called up.'

'I thank you kindly,' said I, 'but I'll not mind it just now; it will be time enough to crop it if I'm appointed.'

'Well, anyhow,' said he, 'hould up your head and don't look any way afeared or daunted when you go up before the Colonel.'

Our conversation was then interrupted, as I was ordered upstairs to appear before the Colonel. As I entered his room, I took off my hat and my brogues, and laid them with my blackthorn on the floor beside me. There was my old friend seated at his desk in all the dignity of office. After he had taken a good long look at me, he said – 'It was you, I think, who brought me this letter from Mr Le Fanu?'

'It was, my lord.'

'You want to go into the police?'

'That's my ambition, your raverance.'

'Can you read and write?'

'Why not, your worship? Sure I got a nate edication.'

'Well, read that,' said he, handing me a letter, which I began to read as follows: 'Sir, I am anxious to become a member of the M-E … me, T-R-O … tro, P-O … Ah begorra, my lord,' said I, 'that long word bates me!'

'Never mind,' he said. 'It is "metropolitan". Go on.'

I got through the rest of the letter swimmingly.

'Take him down now,' said he, 'and have him measured, and then bring him back here.'

I was taken down and put under the measuring instrument, where I kept bobbing up my head to make myself taller.

'Keep quiet, will you,' said the sergeant, putting his hand on my head. 'You have a wig on.'

'Of course I have,' said I.

'Remove it at once,' said he.

'No, nor the dickens a taste,' said I. 'Didn't ye hear the Colonel tellin' me not to dare to take off that wig be reason of a cowld I have in my head.'

So I was measured with my wig on, due allowance being, no doubt, made for it, and was marched up to the Colonel again.

'Exactly six foot, sir,' said the sergeant.

The Colonel then said to me, 'You are to attend here on Friday morning next, at ten o'clock, to be examined by the doctor; and you may tell Mr Le Fanu that if you pass the doctor, I intend to put you into the B division.'

'Long may your honour live!' said I; then, handing him one of my visiting cards, I added: 'Mr Le Fanu bid me give you that.'

'Where is Mr Le Fanu?' said he.

'Here, your raverance,' said I.

'What do you mean?' he asked me.

'Ah, then, Colonel dear, you ould villain, look at me now. Is because I'm in these plain clothes you purtind not to know me?'

Up he jumped, put his arm in mine, and for some minutes laughed so heartily that he could not say a word, while the sergeant and the orderly stood near the door in amazement, thinking we had both gone off our heads. As soon as he could speak he said, 'Come to dine at half past seven, and we'll talk about the B division.'

I ran downstairs to the hall, where candidates came about me, asking, 'Are you appointed?'

'Appointed, ye blackguards of the world!' said I. 'Appointed, is it? I'm not only appointed but, begorra, I'm to dine with the Colonel.'

Superintendent Daniel Ryan

Superintendent Daniel Ryan was born in Philipstown (modern-day Daingean), County Offaly in 1818. A carpenter by trade, he joined F division of the DMP in 1840. He quickly rose through the ranks to take charge of Dublin Castle's G or detective division. His rise was attributable to hard work, and he built his career on some key cases. He and his brother James retired from the force in 1874 to their home in Rowan House, Blackrock, where they lived with their respective wives. In May 1868 Ryan wrote a report of his own volition for the chief secretary of Ireland to support his request for an increased allowance. In writing, his intention was undoubtedly to cast himself in as positive a light as possible. Nevertheless, it represents a rare insight into the day-to-day life of a commanding police officer during the height of the Fenian troubles.[1]

In a celebrated case known as the Jack in the Box case, when a series of extensive robberies were being committed in the Steam Packet and Railway Stores by a contrivance as ingenious and original as it was

Mounted police were an impressive and imposing sight on the streets of Dublin. (*Journal Universel*, 1867)

difficult to detect, I succeeded in making the thief amenable and at the preliminary investigations, J. W. O'Donnell Esq., the present Chief Magistrate, wrote the following remark – 'I beg very respectfully to recommend to the favourable consideration of the Commissioners of Police, their very efficient officer (Acting Inspector D. Ryan). He has displayed throughout this most extraordinarily complicated case the greatest degree of foresight, intelligence and thought. Serving in a great measure if not entirely, to his sagacity and persevering execution, an immense amount of valuable property has been discovered and secured for its respective owners and I feel in consequence I am only doing him an act of justice in bringing his conduct in the case full specially under the notice of the Commissioners'.

My appointment in charge of the division increased my responsibility and did not lessen my labour as I had to apply a certain amount of training to young men under my charge in order to make them efficient and as any mistake on my part in the public interest would be placed to my credit, no arrest of any importance whatsoever was made, save by my directions and under my immediate guidance. About the time of my appointment to the charge of the division, Mr Little was murdered at the Broadstone Railway Terminus and I was specially employed in the case.

I was obliged then, in the interests of the Government to pay particular attention to political matters which about this time were being much talked of in Ireland – the establishment of the National Brotherhood of St Patrick was the principal affair that I had to deal with first. I had to learn all the particulars in regard to its organisation, its plans and to watch the proceedings of meetings and report results.

During the years 1862 and 1863, occasional reports were sufficient to show the Government what was going on but after the establishment of the *Irish People* in November 1863 and thence almost to the present date, I found it necessary to report daily – several times some days – what was to my knowledge in respect of the progress of the newspaper, the object sought to be attained by its managers, their character and position in connection with the Fenian conspiracy, the names of their agents in the provinces, the establishment of supposed drill rooms, the general system of organising, especially in regard to the army to which I was the first to call attention.

After this first blow was given to the conspiracy, it was presumed by the public that there was an end to it but as I took cognisance of the great influx of strangers from America and England, I was enabled to show the Government that the general impression was erroneous as regards the effect of the first Fenian arrests. On account of this great influx of strangers in February 1866, the Government suspended the Habeas Corpus and at about ten o'clock on the night of 16 February, orders were conveyed to me to arrest by virtue of that suspension such persons as were known to me to be here without any lawful business and by eleven o'clock the next morning, I had ninety-one such persons in custody.

I presume it is unnecessary for me to say that without exceptions, those arrests [for Fenianism] were made by my special directions. Consequently, my entire time was of necessity devoted to this business as indicated by the fact that on the occasion of the seizure of the *Irish People* newspaper, I was obliged to remain in this office five days and nights consecutively and a similar time on the occasion of the Habeas Corpus suspensions, my food having been brought to me to the office. While those arrests were under consideration, I felt it necessary to remain in the office until midnight every night, Sunday as well, sifting the various pieces of private information communicated to me and to this extraordinary attentions, I attributed the fact that upon every subsequent inquiry and from what transpired among many of them in prison, it became more manifest that I was not mistaken in any of those I had arrested and that my conduct was not likely to reflect on the administration of the Government.

On the occasion [of the 1867 Fenian rising], I was obliged to remain in the office for ten days and nights consecutively without any opportunity of going to rest in bed, a circumstance in itself sufficient to impair a more youthful and vigorous constitution than mine could be after twenty-eight years police service, yet in the interest of the Government, I persevered because I was perfectly satisfied that there were persons supplying important private information through me who would not communicate with any person who might be appointed to succeed me. They had such a thorough dread of being exposed and knew so much about how the conspirators arrived at information supplied to the Government. It was not until after it had transpired on the witness table that Nagle (the *Irish People* informer) was two years in communication with me without a shadow of suspicion having fallen on him that extraordinary confidence was placed in me by persons who otherwise would have withheld private information but they declared that to their own knowledge, the conspirators never could obtain the names of my informants.

From 1863 to the present, or during the past five years, I frequently had to meet those persons in out of the way places at the most unseasonable hours of the night and although it frequently occurred to me that perhaps a trap was laid for me in some of those places, I kept my appointments at the risk of my life because, as my informants should see me alone,

I could not bring any of my officers with me as protection. The inconvenience and hardships arising out of this particular duty extended to my entire family because I could have no idea when I should meet any of those persons and as a matter of course, my return home would be looked for at the usual hour but in the meantime I received word to be at a certain place and should go there, consequently my family would be disappointed – even their meals would be irregular and of little use to them and after having watched for my arrival until far into the night, they would conclude that I was assassinated, such alarming summons having been in circulation, besides, I received so many threatening letters.

Another duty, perhaps the most critical of all arising out of Fenianism and imposed on me, was the safekeeping of all the Crown witnesses, Nagle to Corydon and Massey, who were arrived in Dublin and as far as I am aware, this duty was carried out to the entire satisfaction of the Crown and the various witnesses, the most difficult to please of them never having made any complaint to my knowledge. Although this political duty might be considered sufficient to task the energies of any man in my position, still I never committed the other duties of the department in respect to the regular of hackney carriages and searching for stolen property, to be neglected and as a proof of this, I may state that the public never complained of any neglect in this respect. From time to time, the most experienced officers of the department were on the sick list on account of their perpetual fatigue in duty they were engaged on, so that previous to the augmentation of the division, the average number of available men I had to assist me in the performance of all this duty did not exceed twelve. Having not taken all the nourishment my salary enabled me to procure, there is no moral doubt if I was not altogether broken up and unfit for further service, I should have had at least succumbed to temporary illness for at this moment, I feel that the past five years have had a worse effect on my constitution than the twenty-three that preceded them.

In conclusion, it may not be out of place to observe that when I was taking charge of Crown witness Massey, the right honourable, the Chief Secretary (Lord Mayo) was pleased to say to me in his room at the Castle that when all would be over, if matters passed off quietly in the meantime, I would not be forgotten. Relying on his word and honour and on the desire always manifested by her Majesty's Government to mark their special recognition of valuable service to the State, I most respectfully place the matter in your hands, perfectly satisfied that my claims shall receive through you the full and fair consideration they may appear to deserve. I am your right humble servant, Daniel Ryan.

Surgeon Richard Butcher

Born on 21 April 1816, Richard Butcher was the son of Vice Admiral Samuel Butcher and Elizabeth Anne Herbert. He spent his childhood years in Danesfort House, a stately home overlooking Lough Leane in Killarney near the River Flesk. He was one of thirteen children and established a fine surgical career in adult life. Among his many accomplishments, he held office as president of the Royal College of Surgeons as well as being a regius professor at Trinity College. An innovator in his own right, Butcher was best known for his modification to the common surgical saw. In addition to orthopaedic surgery, he treated various cancers, cleft lip and palate problems, kidney disorders and cases of drowning, accident and assault. He was a noted Dublin wit who was proud of his muscular arms, strengthened in the boxing ring, where he once gave a good account of himself against the English champion Jem Mace. His medical casebooks are kept at Mercer's Library, Dublin and comprise a number of small volumes written between 1846 and 1859. Mercer's Hospital, where he worked, admitted sick and wounded members of the force on a regular basis and this account helps shed further light on their treatment. In 1867 he cared for two DMP constables, Patrick Keena and Stephen Kelly, after they were shot on duty during the early hours of 31 October in Temple Bar. What follows is an extract from his 1867 book On Gunshot Wounds and their Treatment.

Police sergeant S. Kelly aged thirty-three was admitted to Mercer's Hospital on 31 October 1867 with Constable Keena at quarter past one in the morning after being shot on the same beat and in the few moments after. On his admission, he was collapsed to the lowest degree, almost pulseless, tottering in his gait, even between the steady support of two powerful men who sustained him.

His moans were subdued and altogether suppressed in a remarkable way. On his being questioned, his sufferings were not of that acute terrible description which harassed his fellow

Mr. BUTCHER ON GUN-SHOT WOUNDS.

CASE OF KELLY.

Fig. I.—Showing where the Bullet entered.

Fig. II.—Showing position of Wound made for extraction of Ball.

Mr Oldham's woodcut from Richard Butcher's *On Gunshot Wounds and Their Treatment* (1867).

sufferer, compelling him to scream out wildly and even madly at times.

On being stripped and most carefully examining the body, no second wound could be discovered and the point of entrance of the bullet was a small transverse slit, three quarters of an inch above the extremity of the ensiform cartilage. The edges were not inverted and were cut … For several days, his condition did not vary much from that of his injured companion. There was the same tendency to die by sinking and prostration and there was the same energetic means and constant application of dry heat to the surface, the administration of stimulants and sedatives & c. as often and as persistently as symptoms would permit of as in the former instance. Urine had to be drawn off and so the bladder relieved.

On the fourth day after his admission and on the 4 October, I had the man removed to the next ward, bed and all, so he did not suffer the slightest shake or disturbance. I acted so, in order that he might not be a witness of the dying scene which just hung over his companion. He thus was saved and escaped from the additional depressing agency of such a trial. The man was so little alive himself that he made no comment on the change of place, but lay calm and quiet, staring vacantly upon the ceiling. However, he was alive and without any marked complications, though as depressed still and sunken as compatible with life …

13 November 1867

9 a.m.

Pain checked altogether and the man had a fair quantity of sleep. Detected now for the first time some little fullness between the eighth and ninth ribs on the right side and posteriorly behind the great curves, moderate distension of the corresponding intercostal muscles and to very delicate touch, some slight, deep oedema. This region was likewise more dull on percussion and now vesicular respiration in the lung on the right side was heard very feebly and very deep within.

This important change, as I discovered, was borne testimony to by the most careful examination of our distinguished physician of the hospital, Dr. Moore.

Now, my watchfulness for several days was directed towards this locality as the most probable lurking place of the bullet.

The pain referred in this direction, though not exactly to the spot, on more than two occasions, the discolouration which appeared and so rapidly again passed away.

The injury inflicted on the man's clothes where torn by the bullet and [by] the crushing of the button even in a particular direction; all, it must be admitted, very separate links; yet when connected leading towards a particular inference – that taken by me, as to this being the site in which the ball would be found. Treatment as on yesterday.

4 p.m.

Pain relieved entirely; bowels quiet. Carefully, I examined again for the ball. Kneeling beside the patient's bed, I passed my left hand very gently over the suspected part of the chest and then, with the index finger of my right hand, carried gently from before, backwards along the eighth and ninth intercostal spaces and corresponding to that part already marked out by auscultation and percussion as somewhat dull; by the slightest palpation with the finger between the eighth and ninth ribs, just behind their great curve.

I thought I could discover within the chest, a solid body. Twice I got the slight shock to my finger so as to make me certain that the foreign body was within; small, weighty and moveable. After these very gentle efforts, the foreign body eluded me altogether and the best directed touch could not discover its presence.

9 p.m.
Free from pain; pulse 115; patient a little flushed. Wound suppurating healthily. All sloughed part cast off; chest and abdomen covered with stupes and French wadding and oiled silk as before. Opium continued; all nutriment given tepid and even warm.

14 November 1867
Still flushed; pulse 112; bowels freed; no return of blood. Wound healthy. No pain in its vicinity. Again examined carefully the affected side. No discolouration or increased oedema. No extension of dullness or want of respiratory murmur; as by an application of the same delicate tact as pursued on last evening, I again discovered the same weighty tap from within, on gentle palpation over the suspected spot. This sensation was likewise appreciated by my able colleagues – Drs Moore and Ledwich; yet quietly again the ball hid itself and could be no more felt.

I rolled the patient the least degree, from off of his back, over towards the sound side, not more than three inches, when the foreign body eluded all further detection; neither was it to be discovered on the patient being brought back again to his former position.

To continue opium, stimulants, nutriment.

4 p.m.
I could not discover the foreign body in the most careful and gentle examination.

9 p.m.

Having again made search for the foreign body, I discovered it as distinctly as on the second time, no doubt within the chest, and with some range of motion permitted to it. Mostly likely chambered off from the general pleural cavity.

15 November 1867

The man had a restless night. Pulse 116; skin hot; face flushed and refused his food. I again examined carefully the chest but could obtain no information as to the presence of the foreign body. As satisfactory as before. Continue treatment.

4 p.m.

At this visit, I again felt the weighty little body by the same gentle palpation, very deep and with the gentlest touch, I could satisfy myself of its form. I pronounced it without doubt to be the bullet.

The man made a slight change in his position and again it was gone and hid itself so that it could not be found out. However, I was satisfied that the bullet was there and determined if I again got the same evidence though involving so weighty a question, at once to cut down upon it and accomplish its extraction. However this opportunity was not permitted to me, either at this time or when I again visited my patient at 9 p.m. and I may state at this last hour, I could not satisfy myself, even of its being there.

16 November 1867

On this day, the sixteenth after the accident, I extracted the ball from Kelly's chest at twelve o'clock. For the past three days, I was cognisant of some solid material floating about; easily disturbed from its position and situated far back on the right side of the chest, corresponding to the region behind the greatest curve of the ribs and between the eighth and ninth ribs. On palpation, it was to me evident that there was some little fullness in front of this, corresponding to the blood-discoloured mark before alluded to as being present on the right side.

I determined now to cut down on this point, where I supposed the bullet lay, and returned to the ward to do so at half past nine a.m.

The patient could not be stirred from the bed without a fatal risk. We therefore drew down the bed from the wall and turned it, with the affected side of the patient towards the window. The patient was then gently turned for nearly half a turn towards his left side, but it was now difficult to be certain of the presence of the ball; therefore for the time, further proceeding was abandoned.

I was compelled to desist from the sinking state of the man, from terror in his enfeebled state at the prospect of an operation. A full dose of brandy was given to him in hot water and the patient was allowed to remain in his bed, placed in the same position, opposite to the window, as I intended to return after a little while when his fright passed away and his pulse got up.

At twelve o'clock, I again met my colleagues, as I was not

satisfied in allowing the ball to remain lodged any longer. I gently now turned the patient over, less than half a turn and had him sustained so by his systems. Having now distinctly felt the ball, I cut down upon it in a line corresponding to the course of the ribs and midway between the eighth and ninth and somewhat nearer to the upper edge of the eighth.

The incision was about three inches and a half deep, through the integuments and external layers of intercostal muscles. In the second cut, deeper through the internal layer, an adventitious material – fully a tablespoonful – of purulent matter escaped and some coagulated blood with it. I then pressed steadily upon the part and the bullet presented its convex end and was readily drawn out. But little matter followed its extraction.

I put my finger into the wound and gently searched around. A very considerable cavity; quite smooth on the surface next [to] the lung, but somewhat uneven externally or towards the ribs. The full length of the index finger could range this cavity. I am certain it did not communicate with the right pleural cavity or it may have been a part of it, walled off by adhesions to the visceral layer. This, I believe, is what really took place; or in other words, the pathological change in assisting the ball in its escape from detection during several examinations, yet always retaining it within certain bounds so that it could again be found.

I have mentioned having searched carefully this cavity; my chief object being to ascertain if any foreign bodies, a piece of cloth, the missing top of the button or some other portion of the man's dress had been carried in before the bullet in its rapid course. Such, happily, was not the case. There was no bleeding from the wound.

I placed a few shreds of lint, steeped in oil within the track of the wound, so as to allow any fluid secreted within, readily and at once to escape. A small lint compress was placed on either side of the wound and the parts supported with a few wide strips of adhesive plaster so as to prevent undue motion of the ribs and wounded parts.

The man was much elated on the extraction of the ball, yet to prevent syncope [a faint], brandy had to be freely given. The ball was somewhat flattened in its caul where it struck the button. It also had stamped on it the first two letters of the word 'Police' which was on the button and also some of the internal copper layer of the button impacted brightly on its surface. In a deep groove on one side of the ball lay compressed tightly a small piece of the cloth of the man's coat. The ball was similar in size, weight and form to that which I extracted from the body of Constable Keena shot by the same man and with the same pistol.

Colonel Eamon 'Ned' Broy

Born in 1887, Eamon 'Ned' Broy will be familiar to many readers because of his prominent role in Liam Neeson's Michael Collins *movie. He was a double agent who worked for Collins while also employed by Great Brunswick Street's detective division, and as a result he was able to copy and smuggle out many sensitive police files. In real life Broy was not killed as a result of these activities but lived until 1972. Here he recounts his time as a young recruit with the DMP.*[2]

I joined the DMP Depot in January, 1911. At that time the half year spent in the Depot did not constitute service in the force, which commenced only on the completion of training, and so no oath was administered to us on joining the Depot. Inspector Denis Carey was in charge of training and made a most dashing figure in uniform as one would

Walking the beat could be lonely, particularly for new, country-born recruits. It helped to have a sociable disposition. (*Journal Universel*, 1867)

expect from such a world-famous athlete. We found when he was giving instruction in police duties that it was impossible to pay adequate attention to his instruction as we could only contemplate him as a famous athlete and remember his past athletic feats.

Amongst those who joined the Depot with me was Michael Navin. Navin I found to be an athlete and was, in addition, steeped in the lore of Munster athletics of the previous years which had been practically synonymous with world athletics, such a surpassing excellence did athletes from that province attain about the turn of the century. Navin was veritably a living encyclopaedia of athletic history. He was dismissed in 1918 for refusing to arrest some Blackrock youths for drilling. When asked for a reason for his refusal he stated it was due to the 'two laws' obtaining in Ireland by which the British Government connived at drilling and gunrunning by the Ulster Volunteers but tried to suppress similar activities by the Irish Volunteers. The Castle Authorities considered the question of arresting him, but finally decided that such a step would involve them in adverse publicity.

Whilst we were in the Depot a stranger came to stay there as the guest of Mr Carey. He was a stout, prosperous and successful-looking man, about 40 years of age and of decidedly American appearance, very neat on his feet for a man who obviously weighed over 18 stone although less than six feet in height. Navin and I speculated as to who he might be, as it was obvious that a guest staying with Carey must be an athlete. By dint of photographs in athletic publications Navin finally decided that he was John Flanagan, and John Flanagan he turned out to be. So this triple Olympic hammer champion (1900, 1904 and 1908) and world famous figure was staying in our building for a couple of weeks on his final return from America whilst awaiting participation in the forthcoming DMP sports at Ballsbridge.

During this period, Inspector Carey, aware that I was doing athletic training at Ballsbridge grounds at the time, directed me to take a sixteen pounds hammer to the grounds for Mr Flanagan. He handed me a small leather case which was heavy enough but certainly not long enough to contain a four-foot hammer. A textbook on athletics that I had, which was some years old, showed the athletic hammer as a rigid four-foot sledgehammer. As practical jokes in the Depot were quite usual, I feared that Mr Carey was pulling my leg in order to give John Flanagan a good laugh. Accordingly, when I got away from the Depot I opened the case and found therein the modern athletic hammer, the handle of which was of flexible piano wire with a steel handgrip and ball bearing head consisting of a leather centre covered with a sphere of brass. I felt very proud of the honour of bringing a hammer to John Flanagan, something like what one would have felt in bringing a sword to Wolfe Tone in the revolutionary movement. After all, Flanagan was one of the 'patron saints' of Irish athleticism, with his Irish compeers keeping Ireland's prestige high in the world during that lean period in Irish history in the first decade of the 20th century.

That day, for the first time, I saw Flanagan throw the hammer, a heavy man spinning round in the circle and throwing up the dust in a whirl with all the appearance of what is called in the country a 'fairy blast'. The great athlete described for me the wonderful interest in athletics in America and some of his own experiences there, and finished up by presenting me with an autographed photograph of himself in action. I hastened to Navin to tell him about Flanagan and to make him green with envy at my good fortune. Navin was not a bit surprised at my discovery of the modern hammer, of which he was well aware and which he was able to explain had been invented and patented by Flanagan himself years before.

Subsequently I saw Carey and Flanagan practising at

Ballsbridge. Carey was in very good form at the time and passed 160 feet with a couple of throws. Coming in from the field he winked at me and said: 'If I get in a couple of throws like that at the sports I'll give John here a fright.' Flanagan replied calmly: 'Ah, Dinny, I've won by inches in my time.' He was probably referring to his battle with Matt McGrath, James Mitchell and Con Walsh in America.

The DMP sports came on and Flanagan won at about 170 feet, with Carey second some ten feet behind. Shortly afterwards, Flanagan returned to his native Kilmallock to take up farming, telling us he hoped to be there in time to sow his turnips.

In the Depot in my time were Andy O'Neill and Michael Gleeson, who were later to become famous for refusing an order at Howth Road in July, 1914, to disarm the Volunteers returning from the landing of arms at Howth that day. None of us who had known them in the Depot were in the least surprised in 1914 at their refusal. The astonishing thing was that fate should have ordained that they were the first to be called on. Gleeson was a Tipperary man and O'Neill was from the Wexford–Carlow border, where his ancestors participated in the Insurrection of 1798. O'Neill was a weight-thrower and boxer, weighing 15½ stone, trained, and neither drank nor smoked, so that he must have been physically the most powerful man present that day at Howth Road of all those assembled there whether Volunteers, police or British soldiers.

In the Depot we all fearlessly and openly discussed the national question and it was the first place I heard the song

'The Men of the West'. The majority of us expressed strong national views but there was, to our surprise, a small minority whose views were diametrically opposed to national aspirations. However, we felt that in the event of police opposition to Home Rule, as was forecast, we would have no small say in enforcing the national will no matter who would be against us. I remember one of the recruits who held anti-national views saying in the presence of O'Neill that he would oppose the coming of Home Rule. Andy replied to him, 'Just imagine a ...... like you trying to prevent Home Rule coming. You would be torn into small pieces.'

As I have said, unlike in the case of the RIC, recruits were not sworn in on joining the DMP Depot but only on completion of training. Whilst in the Depot we were taught what the Oath would be, something to the effect of serving without fear or favour, etc., but there was a proviso something to the following effect, viz. 'I swear that I do not now belong to, and that whilst serving I shall not belong to, any secret society whatsoever, the Society of Freemasons excepted.' We thought that it was a great piece of presumption to have that in an oath in Ireland in the 20th century. They might have got away with it in the previous century but not in our time. When the time for swearing in came, recruits were sworn in in batches of about 20 and several of us neither touched the Bible nor repeated the words. Later on in 1919 when a police union was formed, it was successful in removing the offensive section in the oath and in having the time in the Depot counted in total service. ...

Police law and practice were much the same as in London. Constables were armed with batons. All were trained in the use of the revolver, but not the rifle. As was the practice in England, every endeavour was made to avoid the use of the revolver as far as possible, and stringent regulations were laid down to prevent a too ready tendency to use firearms, which should only be resorted to in extreme cases. In order to comply strictly with the regulations regarding shooting, it was practically necessary for city police to be fired on first before being free to shoot. As was said by some of them at the time, 'you would need to make a dying declaration before firing in order to be legally safe'.

All Metropolitan Police stations, uniformed and detective, were lined up by the old ABC private telegraph, to be superseded later on by the telephone. It was possible to send a message simultaneously to all stations by the telegraph system, and copies of all messages were written on special forms for permanent record. The reports of all crimes, articles lost and found, arrests etc., were centralised in the G Division and carefully indexed for instant reference. If a man were shot or a house burgled in, say, Dalkey, within a couple of minutes of the police there receiving the report, it would be received by private telegraph by the police in, say, Crumlin or Clontarf, as well as by the Detective Office.

I was appointed to E Division (uniformed service), which controlled roughly the area between the Grand Canal and the Dodder, which suited me admirably for athletic training owing to the numerous sports grounds in that area. I was, consequently, successful in winning several sprints and high jumps in Dublin and England between 1911 and 1914.

During all this time Home Rule and the Ulster question furnished the main topic of conversation. The great majority of the younger DMP men, but not those in higher ranks, were in favour of Home Rule. The Curragh Mutiny came as a shock to some of the senior officers, who gravely shook their heads, saying that the military cut the ground from under all law and order. Orange members could see nothing wrong in the Curragh affair as they were all 'loyal', whatever that might mean. Some of the younger men were delighted, one saying, 'By God, two parties can play at that game.'

20

THE LEGACY
OF THE DMP

When the Irish Free State was founded in 1922, arrangements were made to disband the semi-militarised RIC in the countryside, and that eventually happened on 4 April that year, under the terms of the Anglo-Irish Treaty. The DMP remained for a little longer, until 5 April 1925, when it was eventually amalgamated into An Garda Síochána. Part of the explanation for its continued existence after the Treaty came into effect may have been contemporary public opinion. Historian Anastasia Dukova, referring to Minister for Justice Kevin O'Higgins' remark that the DMP had been 'a popular force', argues that it never incurred the same abhorrence as the RIC had. As a result, there was no call for it to be disbanded.[1]

When Michael Staines, the first commissioner of the newly formed Civic Guard (which was later renamed An Garda Síochána), said that his men would police by moral authority rather than by strength of arms or numbers, he was in effect echoing the sentiments of Assistant Commissioner John Mallon, who in July 1893 stated of his beloved DMP, 'The only arms we carry are the baton and the arms which nature has given us.'[2] The name Garda Síochána, translated into English, literally means 'Guardians of the Peace', a Gaelicised link to the Peace Officers of the 1820s.

Aside from such moral contiguity, the DMP has also left behind an important cultural legacy. As a child, I remember my maternal grandmother, born in 1914, singing the words of Harrigan and Braham's popular ballad:

When first I came to Dublin town
'Twas in eighteen eighty-three
I went direct, with me head erect
For to join the DMP
Me majestic feet woke Kevin Street
As I walked up proud and free
For well I knew they could not do
Without me, MORIARITY
I'm a well-known bobby of the stalwart squad
I belong to the DMP
And the girls all cry as I pass by
Are you there MORIARITY?[3]

My grandmother, who lived upstairs in an old terraced house, shouted down the last line of the refrain 'Are you there MORIARITY?' as a kind of playful cant, exactly the same way that the character of Joxer Daly uses it in Sean O'Casey's *Juno and the Paycock* – in other words, upon the arrival of a visitor.[4] The song was written in 1876 and was sung by Edward Harrington in a policeman's uniform. Later, Burl Ives accredited the enduring popularity of the ballad to its being sung by rebel and Irish tenor Gerard Crofts in the internment camps that were set up after the 1916 Rising.[5]

A family friend of my grandmother, a retired guard, used to call to her house when I was growing up, and I enjoyed listening to the stories he told about his time on the force. The conversation often turned to my grandmother's childhood visits to Dublin. Back then Ireland was not yet an independent state, and tall DMP constables still stood on street corners. Nelson's Pillar, 'the head place for everyone to meet', left a lasting impression on her, as did the white-gloved policemen directing traffic and making way for the clanging trams leaving for the suburbs.

Tom Hunt, a local policeman, visited her house in Clara on a regular basis to play cards. She told me that one day, beginning to despair of ever issuing a prosecution, he went to a farmer's field and quietly drove out all the cattle. After waiting to make sure that the animals were far enough along the road and getting into every place they shouldn't be, the policeman knocked on the half door. 'Are those your cattle?' he asked, knowing well he had let them out himself. 'I suppose they are,' answered the flustered farmer, who stood scratching his head. Once Tom had a summons for the court, he went back to playing twenty-five.

There was something timeless about those reminiscences, told across an old fireside with an outside toilet in the yard and an ancient Belfast sink in the kitchen.

Not all my memories are positive, however. Growing up

in Dublin's north inner city during the 1980s, I also saw quite a bit of antipathy towards the gardaí, and I can remember being stopped just a stone's throw from my house and asked to turn out my pockets by two officers in a passing squad car. I hadn't done anything wrong, but I remember the feeling of humiliation when, in response to an innocent question, one of them told me 'I am the law' – surely a far cry from Kevin O'Higgins' philosophy: 'The garda do not rule. They are simply the medium through which the people rule.'[6] Thus, when I was fourteen years old the Community Relations Gardaí at Fitzgibbon Street Station took a group of us to the police training centre in Templemore, County Tipperary for the day. I can remember the gym, with knotted ropes hanging down from the ceiling which we did our best to shimmy up.

In many ways, today's police officers are following the same well-worn footsteps as thousands of DMP constables before them. Around College Green one can still recognise the familiar 'B' insignia on the epaulettes of gardaí on bikes as they pass by, and I remember a friendly, white-moustachioed officer on traffic duty who used to give me a friendly wave every morning as I cycled to work over Chapelizod Bridge. In every respect, he was the very embodiment of the city's policemen of old. On another occasion I remember watching a new recruit being trained on traffic duty one day at the junction of South Great George's Street and Dame Street. He semaphored the various hand signals while a more experienced officer looked on. 'Eyes front,' he was telling him. 'Eyes front.'

When I was in my late teens I applied to the Garda Band and

got an interview. In effect, this would have meant me joining the force. At that time I played euphonium in the SIPTU brass and reed band, and once a year we used to march to the James Connolly memorial at Arbour Hill. We played at a couple of union disputes – one of them outside a bread factory in the pouring rain – and I can remember what it felt like to march on the streets and play in the city's old bandstands, particularly during the summer in St Stephen's Green when the breeze threatened to blow our music sheets away. Although I didn't realise it then, the DMP musicians of yesteryear had sat in the very same spot. When I went up to the Phoenix Park, I played a piece of music and was then taken away to have my height taken. I fell just short of the requirement. Some traditions don't change, I suppose; perhaps, like W. R. Le Fanu, I should have bobbed up my head to appear taller.

A modern, organised police force has existed in Dublin in one form or another for almost two centuries. It is an essential part not just of our past but of our modern capital city. The city may, like the Pete St John ballad, 'go on changing', but as long as human nature persists, with all its eccentricities and drama, we will always need the Peelers.

ENDNOTES

Introduction

1 http://www.dippam.ac.uk/eppi/documents/13652/download.

2 Joseph V. O'Brien, *Dear, Dirty Dublin: A City in Distress, 1899–1916* (University of California, Berkeley, 1982), p. 180.

3 'Bill to Amend Provision for the Government of Ireland', 27 July 1893, EPPI, HC 428, Section 29.

4 *The Freeman's Journal*, 9 July 1893.

5 'Dublin Metropolitan Police: Instructions, Orders, Etc.', 1837, National Archives of Ireland (hereafter NAI), CSORP 1837/1719, pp. 5–8.

6 Galen Broeker, *Rural Disorder and Police Reform in Ireland* (Routledge & Kegan Paul, London, 1970), p. 199.

7 *Dublin Evening Mail*, 11 November 1843.

8 *The Freeman's Journal*, 9 July 1893.

9 'Memo of Deputy Inspector General, RIC', 26 March 1892, and 'Memo of Chief Secretary', 1 April 1892, NAI, CBS 1893 7174A/S.

10 *The Freeman's Journal*, 12 January 1891.

1 Walking the Beat

1 James Stephens, *The Charwoman's Daughter* (Scepter Books, Dublin, 1912), p. 22.

ENDNOTES

2 'Dublin Metropolitan Police: Instructions, Orders, Etc.', 1837, NAI, CSORP 1837/1719, pp. 5–8.

3 *Ibid.*

4 Donal P. McCracken, *Inspector Mallon: Buying Irish Patriotism for a Five-Pound Note* (Irish Academic Press, Dublin, 2009), p. 11.

5 Jim Herlihy, *The Dublin Metropolitan Police: A Short History and Genealogical Guide* (Four Courts, Dublin, 2001), p. 105.

6 Official notebook of John Moore, DMP 1354, cited in Herlihy, *The Dublin Metropolitan Police*, p. 41.

7 See: 'Report on Suspicious Strangers in Dublin', 7 January 1898, NAI CSORP 1880/27722.

8 'Report of B Division, College Green', 7 January 1898, NAI CBS 1898/15103.

9 Andrew Reed, *The Irish Constable's Guide* (Alex. Thom & Co., Dublin, 1895), p. 326.

10 *Ibid.*

11 Stephens, *The Charwoman's Daughter*, p. 25.

12 *The Freeman's Journal*, 2 October 1838.

13 'Case of John Bergin, on Revoking of Carriage License 2400 for Ill Treatment of His Children', May 1905, NAI CSORP/10167.

14 'Deposition of Mary MacDonnell, Taken by Magistrate W. W. Lynam', 28 September 1839, NAI CSORP 69/8781 in Carton 3/615/2.

15 'Magistrate Lynam to Dublin Castle', 14 October 1839, NAI CSORP 69/8781 in Carton 3/615/2.

16 *The Freeman's Journal*, 23 April 1859.

17 'Petition of Residents of Temple Street Area to Commissioner of Dublin Metropolitan Police', *c.* 1890, Temple Street Hospital archive.

18 Shin-ichi Takagami, 'The Dublin Fenians: 1858–1879' (unpublished PhD thesis, Trinity College, Dublin, 1990), p. 185.

19 'Abstract of Cases under Habeas Corpus Suspension Act 1866, Vol. II', NAI CSOICR 11.

20 Larcom Papers, 6 August 1868, National Library of Ireland (hereafter NLI) Constabulary Organisation and Duties, MS 7619.

21 Acting Superintendent Ryan to Magistrate O'Donnel, 31 October 1867, NAI CSORP 1867/19343.

22 *The Freeman's Journal*, 22 August 1840.

23 *Ibid.*, 29 July 1842.

24 *Ibid.*, 24 August 1855.

25 Interview with Richard Fitzgerald, September 2002.

26 Interview with Seamus Marken, 26 November 2011.

27 Brian Griffin, 'The Irish Police, 1836–1914: A Social History' (unpublished PhD thesis, University of Chicago, 1991), pp. 750 and 763.

28 Frank Porter, *Gleanings and Reminiscences* (Hodges, Foster and Co., Dublin, 1875), p. 159.

29 Architect William Murray to Robert Roberts, February 1828, NAI CSORP 171/3.

30 NAI CSORP 1883/2204, CSORP 1888/8402 and CSORP 1889/210.

31 Purchase of typewriting machines for Dublin Metropolitan Police, 1 September 1889, NAI CSORP 1889/13365.

2 The Dublin Charleys

1 Thomas King Moylan, 'The Little Green: Part II', in *Dublin Historical Record*, vol. 8, no. 4, September–November 1946, pp. 135–56.

2 'Minute Book of Directors of the Watch', 1750–70, NAI P4960-1.

ENDNOTES

3 W. R. Le Fanu, *Seventy Years of Irish Life, Being Anecdotes and Reminiscences* (Macmillan, New York and London, 1893), p. 86.

4 *The Freeman's Journal*, 6 February 1913.

5 *Finn's Leinster Journal*, 30 December 1775.

6 *The Freeman's Journal*, 19 October 1790. These Irish Volunteers were set up by the government in 1778 as a kind of local militia to guard against invasion.

7 *Ibid.*, 22 June 1780.

8 *Ibid.*, 17 November 1778.

9 *An Account of All Sums of Money Raised by Local Tax or Otherwise for the Support of the Police of the City of Dublin during the Years 1808 and 1809; Together with an Account of the Expenditure Thereof* (London, 1810).

10 Brian Henry, 'Animadversions on the Street Robberies in Dublin, 1765', in *Irish Jurist*, vol. 23, no. 2, Winter 1988, pp. 347–356.

11 *The Freeman's Journal*, 21 April 1785.

12 Kevin P. O'Rorke, 'Dublin Police', in *Dublin Historical Record*, vol. 29, no. 4, September 1976, pp. 138–47.

13 *An Account of all Sums of Money Raised.*

14 Robert Maunsell, *Recollections of Ireland, Collected from Fifty Years Practice and Residence in the Country, By a Late Professional Gentleman* (Dublin, 1865), p. 37.

15 Irish Statute Book, 'Dublin Police Act 1836', http://www.irish statutebook.ie/eli/1836/act/29/enacted/en/print.html.

16 Anastasia Dukova has also alluded to this in *A History of the Dublin Metropolitan Police and Its Colonial Legacy* (Palgrave Macmillan, London, 2016), p. 45. She points out that 'not all watchmen were equally easy prey' for tricksters and thieves.

17 Dublin Metropolitan Police General Register, Garda Museum and Archives. The entry for John Fitzpatrick, Kanturk, County Cork can be found under warrant number 136.

3 The Night of the Big Wind

1 Frank Watters, 'The Night of the Big Wind', in *Journal of the Poyntzpass and District Local Society*, no. 7, May 1994, pp. 73–82.

2 *Dublin Evening Packet*, 12 January 1839.

3 *Ibid.*

4 *Leinster Express*, 19 January 1839.

5 *The Freeman's Journal*, 8 January 1839.

6 *Leinster Express*, 19 January 1839.

7 *Ibid.*

8 Estimate of damage done in storm, NAI CSORP 1839/4.

9 *Ibid.*

10 Report of Constable 87C, 7 January 1839, NAI CSORP 1839/4.

11 *The Freeman's Journal*, 15 January 1839.

4 Strange Crimes and Unusual Punishments

1 *The Nation*, 8 February 1873.

2 *Ibid.*

3 Superintendent Ryan to Chief Secretary, 22 June 1868, NAI CSORP 1868/5237.

4 Jerry White, *London in the Nineteenth Century: A Human Awful Wonder of God* (Random House, London, 2007), p. 336.

5 *The Nation*, 18 May 1872.

6 *The Freeman's Journal*, 23 May 1872.

7 *Ibid.*, 25 November 1862.

8   NAI CSORP 1895/19097.

9   *The Irish Times*, 7 October 1907.

10 Barry Kennerk, *Shadow of the Brotherhood: The Temple Bar Shootings* (Mercier Press, Cork, 2010), p. 180.

11 Griffin, 'The Irish Police, 1836–1914', pp. 759, 766 and 771.

12 Barry Kennerk, Kennerk family history, unpublished.

13 Griffin, 'The Irish Police, 1836–1914', pp. 750 and 763.

5 One of the Last Duels in Ireland

1   *Dublin Almanac and General Register of Ireland for 1847*, p. 233.

2   *Bell's Life in Sydney and Sporting Chronicle*, 13 August 1864.

3   *Dublin Almanac and General Register of Ireland for 1847*.

4   Le Fanu, *Seventy Years of Irish Life*, p. 141.

5   *The Freeman's Journal*, 3 June 1839.

6   *Ibid.*

7   Le Fanu, *Seventy Years of Irish Life*, p. 143.

8   Hugh Kenner, *A Sinking Island: The Modern English Writers* (Knopf, New York, 1988), p. 19.

6 Raining Cats, Dogs and Other Animals

1   *The Nation*, 19 October 1844.

2   *Kerry Evening Post*, 9 June 1849.

3   *The Nation*, 15 April 1848.

7 Policing in All Weathers

1   George Moore, *A Drama in Muslin: A Realistic Novel* (W. Scott, London, 1893).

2   Dan Milner, *Irish Pirate Ballads and Other Songs of the Sea*

(Smithsonian Folkways, Washington, 2009).

3   Cited in the *Leinster Express*, 18 February 1854.

4   *Dublin Quarterly Journal of Medical Science*, vol. VII, February and May 1849.

5   *Ibid.*

6   Murder of Constable Carrigee, NAI CSORP 1896/16020.

7   'Duties of the Resident Pupils of the Richmond Surgical Hospital', NAI Board of Governors Minutes 9 April 1868–22 June 1871, House of Industry Hospitals.

8   NAI CSORP 1881/40176 and CSORP 1882/37709.

9   *The Dublin Magazine*, vol. 17–18, p. 3.

10 *Saunders Newsletter*, 21 January 1868.

11 Acting Superintendent Ryan to CP, 24 November 1867, NAI CSORP, 1867/20446/1867 in carton 175.

12 *The Irish Times*, 22 December 1934.

8 Grave Robbers and Crooked Coroners

1   Anatomy Act file, NAI CSORP 1839/33/3293 in Carton 3/615/2 (this comprises quite a large file on the subject of anatomy schools in Dublin during this period).

2   'Report of Officer J. Gamble, Cork to Inspector General of RIC', 4 March 1839, NAI CSORP 1839/33/1262 in Carton 3/615/2.

3   *The Freeman's Journal*, 14 January 1839.

4   *The Cork Examiner*, 25 April and *The Freeman's Journal*, 30 March 1842.

5   *Dublin Medical Press*, 17 August 1842.

6   Frank Thorpe Porter, *Gleanings and Reminiscences* (Hodges, Foster, & Co., Dublin, 1875), p. 76.

7   *The Freeman's Journal*, 9 April 1869.

8   *Ibid.*

9   Dublin City Council Minutes, 24 March 1865 (Gilbert Library, C1/A1/26, 27).

10 Dublin City Council Minutes, 29 March 1866 (Gilbert Library, C1/A1/26, 27).

11 Dublin City Council Minutes, January 1870–February 1871, Dublin City Library and Archive, C2/A1/31.

12 Robert Welch, *The Abbey Theatre, 1899-1999: Form and Pressure* (Oxford University Press, Oxford, 1999), p. 179.

9 Zozimus and Constable 184B

1   Gulielmus (Dubliniensis Humoriensis), *Memoir of the Great Original, Zozimus (Michael Moran), the Celebrated Dublin Street Rhymer and Reciter* (M'Glashan & Gill, Dublin, 1871), p. 7.

2   *The Freeman's Journal*, 7 September 1844.

3   P. J. McCall, 'Zozimus', in *Dublin Historical Record*, vol. 7, no. 4, September–November 1945, pp. 134–149.

4   *Ibid.*

5   *Ibid.*

6   Gulielmus (Dubliniensis Humoriensis), *Memoir of the Great Original, Zozimus (Michael Moran)*, p. 7.

7   *Ibid.*

8   George Dennis Zimmermann, *Irish Political Street Ballads and Rebel Songs, 1780–1900* (Imprimerie La Sirène, Genève, 1966), p. 220.

9   Gulielmus (Dubliniensis Humoriensis), *Memoir of the Great Original, Zozimus (Michael Moran)*, p. 20.

10 *The Cork Examiner*, 1 November 1844.

11 *Kerry Examiner*, 22 October 1844.

12 *The Freeman's Journal*, 1 November 1844.

13 *Ibid.*, 31 July 1844.

14 *Ibid.*, 6 June 1842.

15 *Ibid.*, 24 October 1840.

16 *Ibid.*, 8 December 1841.

17 *Ibid.*, 28 March 1845.

10 The Last King of Mud Island

1 *The Freeman's Journal*, 21 July 1825.

2 *Ibid.*, 26 September 1843.

3 This saying was originally quoted in the aforementioned *Irish Times* article of 4 February 1911 but thereafter was mentioned by many writers, such as Weston St Joyce.

4 'Interment of Christopher McDonnell', June 1852, Prospect Cemetery interment records, 1852/48/1.

5 *The Industries of Dublin, Historical, Statistical, Biographical. An Account of the Leading Business Men, Commercial Interests, Wealth and Growth* (S. Blackett, London, 1887), p. 72.

6 William Wilson, *Modern Plan of the City and Environs of Dublin*, 1798.

7 *The Illustrated Dublin Journal*, 22 March 1862.

8 *The Freeman's Journal*, 20 November 1826.

9 James Wren, 'From Ballybough to Scurlogue's Bridge', in *Dublin Historical Record*, vol. 37, no. 1, December 1983, pp. 14–29.

10 Ireland–Australia Transportation Database, 'Files of Thomas McNally (1837) and John Scott (1847)', http://www.nationalarchives.ie/article/penal-transportation-records-ireland-australia-1788-1868-2/.

11 *The Dublin University Magazine*, no. 2, 1853, p. 402.

12 *The Irish Times*, 4 February 1911.

13 *The Illustrated Dublin Journal*, no. 1, 1862, p. 202.

14 Memorial of an indenture of deed of mortgage, 14 November 1840, reciting an earlier indenture of 14 November 1817 (Registry of Deeds, no. 119).

15 Maunsell and another to McDonnell, registered on 14 December 1840 and reciting various earlier memorials of indenture (Registry of Deeds, 1841/119).

16 *The Irish Times*, 4 February 1911.

17 *Ibid.*

18 *The Freeman's Journal*, 25 July 1826.

19 *Ibid.*, 2 October 1838.

20 *Ibid.*, 9 November 1831.

21 Calendar of Wills and Administrations, 1852, NAI.

22 'Interment of Christopher McDonnell', June 1852, Prospect Cemetery interment records 1852/48/1.

23 Will Books, 1863 and 1864, marriages of Jane McDonnell and Bridget Kearney, née McDonnell, http://www.willcalendars. nationalarchives.ie/search/cwa/index.jsp.

24 Dillon Cosgrave, *North Dublin: City and Environs* (Catholic Truth Society of Ireland, Dublin, 1909), p. 77.

25 See *The Irish Times*, 6 December 1876.

11 An Apache Attack on Parnell Square

1 Interview with Jack Kennerk, 10 September 2018. During the 1940s, pamphlets were issued to every household in Dublin setting out how a new pesticide called DDT should be used to combat lice.

2 *The Freeman's Journal*, 7 June 1886.

3 *Ibid.*, 5 October 1888.

4 *Ibid.*, 18 September 1881.

5 *Ibid.*, 22 December 1892.

12 The Tram-racing Stilt Walker

1 *The Freeman's Journal*, 25 March 1886.

2 *Belfast Newsletter*, 3 November 1885.

3 *Ibid.*, 17 November 1886.

4 Ernest Temple Thurston, *The Forest Fire and Other Stories* (Cassell, London and New York, 1919), p. 143.

5 *The Freeman's Journal*, 26 March 1886.

6 *Ibid.*

7 *Belfast Newsletter*, 30 March 1886.

8 *The Freeman's Journal*, 7 April 1886.

13 The Burgh Quay Tragedy

1 Entry for Constable Patrick Sheahan, Corporation of Dublin Register for Coroner's Court and Morgue, 15 May 1905, NAI CSORP G2/649/44.

2 Record of Patrick Sheahan, warrant number 10032 in Dublin Metropolitan Police General Register, Garda Museum and Archives. According to his record, he was from Ballyguilternan, Glin, County Limerick, where he previously worked as a farmer. He first joined E division on 15 January 1897, and a year later he joined B division.

3 *The Freeman's Journal*, 10 October 1902.

4 *The Irish Times*, 24 March 1904.

5 *Ibid.*, 13 May 1905.

6 *The Cork Examiner*, 8 May 1905.

7 Record of John Sheahan, warrant number 9722 in Dublin Metropolitan Police General Register, Garda Museum and Archives.

8 *The Freeman's Journal*, 13 May 1905.

9 Entry for Constable Patrick Sheahan, Corporation of Dublin Register for Coroner's Court and Morgue, 15 May 1905, NAI CSORP G2/649/44.

10 *The Freeman's Journal*, 9 May 1905.

11 *The Irish Times*, 11 April 1904.

12 *Ibid.*, 2 September 1905.

14 Rabid Dogs

1 *The Freeman's Journal*, 31 July 1879.

2 *The Nature and Treatment of Rabies or Hydrophobia: Being the Report of the Special Commission appointed by the Medical Press and Circular with Valuable Additions* (London, 1878), p. 15.

3 *The Freeman's Journal*, 26 July 1844.

4 A trawl through the Chief Secretary Registered Papers for 1898 shows that there were at least ten such cases in Dublin that year alone (NAI CSORP 1898/2618, 4023, 4338, 7172, 8624, 8816, 9398, 9452, 11837 and 12648).

5 *The Freeman's Journal*, 8 June 1885.

6 *Ibid.*

7 *Evening Herald*, 1 August 1894.

8 *Irish Fireside*, summer edition, June 1885.

9 *The Freeman's Journal*, 12 August 1879.

10 *Evening Herald*, 25 August 1913.

11　Porter, *Gleanings and Reminiscences*, p. 119.

12　*Ibid.*, p. 96.

13　*The Irish Times*, 10 May 1859.

15　A Hog in Armour: The Shooting of Thomas Talbot

1　*The Times*, 18 November 1871.

2　P. J. Tynan, *The Irish National Invincibles and their Times: Three Decades of Struggle Against the Foreign Conspirators in Dublin Castle* (Irish National Invincible Publishing Co., New York, 1894).

3　Roger Joseph McHugh, *Trial at Green Street Courthouse: A Historical Play in Ten Scenes* (Browne and Nolan, Dublin, 1945).

4　A. M., D. B. and T. D. Sullivan, *Speeches from the Dock, or Protests of Irish Patriotism*, Part 1 (Gill, Dublin, 1868), p. 188.

5　Larcom Papers, 1867, NLI MS 7517/332–333.

6　John Hill, *Report of the Trial of Robert Kelly for the Murder of Head-Constable Talbot, at the City of Dublin Commission Court, October, 1871* (Alexander Thom, Dublin, 1873), p. 31.

7　*The Times*, 13 and 14 July 1871, and *The Irish Times*, 13 July 1871.

8　'Duties of the Resident Pupils of the Richmond Surgical Hospital' and Minutes of Board Meeting, 21 May 1868, NAI Arch 7/B.

9　*Proceedings of the Pathological Society of Dublin*, 1868, p. 370.

10　D. J. Bentley, *English Criminal Justice in the Nineteenth Century* (Hambledon Press, London, 1998), p. 217. Due to the high risk of mortality, victims of serious crime in the late nineteenth century were often pressed for information about their attacker at the hospital bedside. In some cases, suspects were even brought before patients in handcuffs or 'darbies'.

11 J. D. H. Widdess, *The Richmond, Whitworth and Hardwicke Hospitals: St. Lawrence's Dublin, 1772–1972* (privately published, Dublin, 1972), p. 128.

12 Harriet C. Frazier, *Slavery and Crime in Missouri, 1773–1865* (McFarland, North Carolina, 2001), p. 43.

13 M. Fallon (ed.), *The Sketches of Erinensis – Selections of Irish Medical Satire, 1824–1836* (Skilton and Shaw, London, 1994), p. 52.

14 R. Harrison and R. Watts, *The Dublin Dissector or Manual of Anatomy* (Samuel S. and William Wood, New York, 1854), p. 477.

15 *The British Medical Journal*, 23 December 1871.

16 *Ibid.*

17 *The Freeman's Journal*, 14 February 1866.

18 *The British Medical Journal*, 23 December 1871.

19 R. Pigott, *Personal Recollections of an Irish National Journalist* (Hodges, Figgis, & Co., Dublin, 1882), p. 369.

20 'W. Armstrong to Chief Secretary, A Division Report', 7 March 1867, NAI CSORP 1867/3822.

21 Griffin, 'The Irish Police, 1836–1914', p. 658.

22 Inspector Hogan (Birmingham) to Dublin Castle, 18 October 1871, NAI Fenian R files, 7753.

23 'Chief Secretary Papers Abstract Book', NAI CSORP 1871/15263.

24 T. D. V. White, *The Road to Excess: A Biography of Isaac Butt* (Browne & Nolan, Dublin, 1946), p. 246.

25 *Report of the Trial of Robert Kelly*, pp. 32 and 112.

26 By the 1860s such displays had become highly contentious, and Louis Lloyd's anatomical museum, based in Leeds, was the first such teaching facility to be prosecuted under the 1857 Obscene

Publications Act. Specimens from gunshot victims continued to find their way into display cases up until the early years of the twentieth century. I am indebted to Dr Bates for this information.

27 White, *The Road to Excess*, p. 258.

28 Head Constable Joseph Murphy to Dublin Castle, 18 October 1871, NAI, Fenian R files, 7753.

29 Superintendent Ryan to CP, 3 May 1866, NAI CSORP 1866/8701.

30 Larcom Papers, Fenianism, 1867, NLI MS 7517, pp. 332–333.

31 Larcom Papers, Fenianism, 1867, NLI MS 7517, p. 332.

16 A Casualty of Dublin's Dynamite War

1 *Belfast Newsletter*, 26 December 1892.

2 *The Irish Times*, 29 December 1892.

3 *Ibid.*

4 Deposition of Samuel George Reeves to Chief Commissioner, Dublin Metropolitan Police, 10 January 1893, NAI CBS 6234/S 1893.

5 *The Irish Times*, 27 December 1892.

6 *Ibid.*, 29 December 1892.

17 The Phoenix Park Deer that Faced a Court Martial

1 Louis O. Mink, *A Finnegan's Wake Gazetteer* (Bloomington, Indiana University Press, 1978), p. 298.

2 Earnan P. Blythe, 'The DMP', in *Dublin Historical Record*, vol. 20, no. 3–4, June–September 1965, pp. 116–126.

3 F. W. Gumley, 'Remembering ...', in *Dublin Historical Record*, vol. 34, no. 2, March 1981, pp. 54–56.

4 *The Irish Times*, 20 November 1861.

5 *Sunday Independent*, 2 February 1908.

6   *The Irish Times*, 15 September 1915.

7   *Ibid.*, 7 February 1917.

8   *Royal Irish Constabulary Magazine,* 1911.

18 Policing a Troubled City

1   *Irish Independent*, 14 August 1913.

2   *The Freeman's Journal*, 18 September 1913.

3   Conor Brady, *Guardians of the Peace* (Gill and Macmillan, Dublin, 1974), p. 17.

4   *The Freeman's Journal*, 12 January 1891.

5   Anastasia Dukova, 'Policing the Lockout: The Role of the DMP', in *History Ireland*, vol. 21, no. 4, July/August 2013, pp. 32–33.

6   John Devoy, *Recollections of an Irish Rebel* (Chase D. Young Company, New York, 1929), p. 204.

7   Report of the Dublin Disturbances Commission, London, 1914.

8   *The Irish Times*, 6 September 1913.

9   Report of the Dublin Disturbances Commission, London, 1914.

10 Entry for James Nolan, Corporation of Dublin Register for Coroner's Court and Morgue, 1 September 1913, NAI G2/649/44.

11 Robert Monteith, *Casement's Last Adventure* (M. F. Moynihan, Dublin, 1953), p. 6.

12 Mrs Sidney Czira witness statement, Irish Military Archives, Bureau of Military History Witness Statement (hereafter BMH WS) 909.

13 *Ibid.*

14 Stephen Prendergast, BMH WS 755.

15 McCracken, *Inspector Mallon*, p. 59.

16 *Evening Herald*, 1 September 1913.

17 Police witness statements, 11 September 1913, NAI CSORP 17743.

18 Report of the Dublin Disturbances Commission, London, 1914.

19 Entries for James Nolan, 1 September 1913 and John Byrne, 5 September 1913, Corporation of Dublin register for Coroner's Court and Morgue, NAI G2/649/44.

20 Dukova, 'Policing the Lockout', p. 135.

21 *Sinn Fein Rebellion Handbook* (Weekly Irish Times, Dublin, 1916), p. 18.

22 John Dillon to Lady Mathew, 'an account of the Rising', 25 April–1 May 1916, TCD, John Dillon Papers, MS 9820.

23 *Sinn Fein Rebellion Handbook*, p. 92.

24 *Ibid.*, p. 75.

25 'Dublin Metropolitan Police Prisoner Book, 1916–1918', UCD archive, Prisoner Book 5.

26 'D. Kennedy, 16 Mary Street Dublin to Chief Commissioner of Police', 23 May 1916, NAI CSORP/5612.

27 *Ibid.*

28 'Inspector John Mills Report, Store Street, C Division', 29 May 1916, NAI CSORP/5612.

29 Gregory Allen, 'Arms, the Dublin Police and the 1916 Rising', September 1977, Garda Museum and Archive.

30 *Ibid.*

31 Henry Robinson, *Memories: Wise and Otherwise* (Cassell, London, 1923), p. 214. See also 'Agitation for Increased Pay of Dublin Metropolitan Police (DMP) and Dismissal of Ringleaders – Inquiry and Report', 1916, National Archives, UK, CO 904/174/4.

32 Gregory Allen, 'Arms, the Dublin Police and the 1916 Rising', September 1977, Garda Museum and Archive.

33 Report of Royal Commission on the circumstances connected with the landing of arms at Howth on 26 July 1914 [Cd 7631], House of Commons, 1914-16, xxiv, 805–20.

19 In Their Own Words: First-hand Accounts of Police Work in Dublin

1 Description by himself of the career of Daniel Ryan, detective in Dublin Castle Service, 1842–1868, NLI, F. S. Bourke Collection, MS 10,744.

2 Eamon Broy, BMH WS 1280.

20 The Legacy of the DMP

1 Anastasia Dukova, *A History of the Dublin Metropolitan Police*, p. 137.

2 *The Freeman's Journal*, 9 July 1893.

3 John Franceschina, *David Braham: The American Offenbach* (Routledge, London and New York, 2003), p. 104.

4 Sean O'Casey, *Juno and the Paycock: A tragedy in three acts* (Samuel French, London, 1932).

5 Royal Irish Constabulary, www.royalirishconstabulary.webs.com.

6 Brady, *Guardians of the Peace*, p. 104.

BIBLIOGRAPHY

Primary Sources

Garda Museum and Archive

Allen, Gregory, 'Arms, the Dublin Police and the 1916 Rising', September 1977

Dublin Metropolitan Police General Register

Glasnevin Museum and Trust

Interment of Christopher McDonnell, King of Mud Island, June 1852 (48/1)

Interviews

Interview with Richard Fitzgerald, September 2002

Interview with Seamus Marken, 26 November 2011

Irish Military Archive

Bureau of Military History Witness Statements

National Archives of Ireland

Chief Secretary Office Registered Papers (1837–1913)

Corporation of Dublin Register for Coroner's Court and Morgue (G2/649/44)

Crime Branch Special Papers

Fenian 'R' Files

BIBLIOGRAPHY

Minute Book of Directors of the Watch, 1750–70 (P4960-1)

Records of the Richmond Hospital (Arch 7/B)

National Library of Ireland

Description by himself of the career of Daniel Ryan, detective in Dublin
Castle Service, 1842–1868 (NLI, F. S. Bourke Collection, MS
10,744)

Thomas Larcom Papers on Fenianism, February 1855–August 1869,
MS 7517

Thomas Larcom Papers, letters and newscuttings related to the
constabulary, 1864–1876, NLI MS 7619

Registry of Deeds

Memorials of Indenture Concerning Various Parties and Christopher
McDonnell, King of Mud Island (1841/119)

Temple Street Children's Hospital Archive

Petition of Residents of Temple Street Area to Commissioner of Dublin
Metropolitan Police, *c*.1890

Trinity College Dublin

John Dillon Papers, MS 9820

University College Dublin Archive

Dublin Metropolitan Police Prisoner Books, 1916–1918

Secondary Sources

*An Account of All Sums of Money Raised by Local Tax or Otherwise for the
Support of the Police of the City of Dublin during the Years 1808 and
1809; Together with an Account of the Expenditure Thereof* (London,
1810)

Bentley, D. J., *English Criminal Justice in the Nineteenth Century* (Hambledon Press, London, 1998)

Blythe, E. P., 'The DMP', in *Dublin Historical Record*, vol. 20, no. 3–4, June–September 1965, pp. 116–126

Brady, C., *Guardians of the Peace* (Gill and Macmillan, Dublin, 1974)

Broeker, G., *Rural Disorder and Police Reform in Ireland* (Routledge & Kegan Paul, London, 1970)

Cosgrave, D., *North Dublin: The North City and Suburbs* (Catholic Truth Society of Ireland, Dublin, 1909)

Devoy, J., *Recollections of an Irish Rebel* (Chase D. Young Company, New York, 1929)

Dukova, A., *A History of the Dublin Metropolitan Police and its Colonial Legacy* (Palgrave Macmillan, London, 2016)

Dukova, A., 'Policing the Lockout: The Role of the DMP', in *History Ireland*, vol. 21, no. 4, July/August 2013, pp. 32–33

Fallon, M. (ed.), *The Sketches of Erinensis – Selections of Irish Medical Satire, 1824–1836* (Skilton and Shaw, London, 1994)

Flint, J., *The Dublin Police, and the Police System* (Dublin, 1847)

Franceschina, J., *David Braham: The American Offenbach* (Routledge, London and New York, 2003)

Frazier, H. C., *Slavery and Crime in Missouri, 1773–1865* (McFarland, North Carolina, 2001)

Griffin, B., 'The Irish Police, 1836–1914: A Social History', unpublished PhD thesis, University of Chicago, 1991

Gulielmus (Dubliniensis Humoriensis), *Memoir of the Great Original, Zozimus (Michael Moran), the Celebrated Dublin Street Rhymer and Reciter* (M'Glashan & Gill, Dublin, 1871)

Gumley, F. W., 'Remembering …', in *Dublin Historical Record*, vol. 34, no. 2, March 1981, pp. 54–56

BIBLIOGRAPHY

Harrison, R. and R. Watts, *The Dublin Dissector or Manual of Anatomy* (Samuel S. and William Wood, New York, 1854)

Henry, B., 'Animadversions on the Street Robberies in Dublin, 1765', in *Irish Jurist*, vol. 23, no. 2, Winter 1988

Herlihy, J., *The Dublin Metropolitan Police: A Short History and Genealogical Guide* (Four Courts, Dublin, 2001)

Hill, J., *Report of the Trial of Robert Kelly for the Murder of Head-Constable Talbot, at the City of Dublin Commission Court, October, 1871* (Alexander Thom, Dublin, 1873)

Kenner, H., *A Sinking Island: The Modern English Writers* (Knopf, New York, 1988)

Kennerk, B., *Shadow of the Brotherhood: The Temple Bar Shootings* (Mercier Press, Cork, 2010)

King Moylan, T., 'The Little Green: Part II', in *Dublin Historical Record*, September–November 1946, pp. 135–56

Le Fanu, W. R., *Seventy Years of Irish Life, Being Anecdotes and Reminiscences* (Macmillan, New York and London, 1893)

Maunsell, Robert, *Recollections of Ireland, Collected from Fifty Years Practice and Residence in the Country, by a late professional gentleman* (Dublin, 1865)

McCall, P. J., 'Zozimus', in *Dublin Historical Record*, vol. 7, no. 4, September–November 1945, pp. 134–149

McCracken, D. P., *Inspector Mallon: Buying Irish Patriotism for a Five-Pound Note* (Irish Academic Press, Dublin, 2009)

McHugh, R. J., *Trial at Green Street Courthouse: A Historical Play in Ten Scenes* (Browne and Nolan, Dublin, 1945)

Mink, L. O., *A Finnegan's Wake Gazetteer* (Bloomington, Indiana University Press, 1978)

Milner, D., *Irish Pirate Ballads and Other Songs of the Sea* (Smithsonian Folkways, Washington, 2009)

Monteith, R., *Casement's Last Adventure* (M. F. Moynihan, Dublin, 1953)

Moore, G., *A Drama in Muslin: A Realistic Novel* (W. Scott, London, 1893)

O'Brien, J. V., *Dear, Dirty Dublin: A City in Distress, 1899–1916* (University of California, Berkeley, 1982)

O'Casey, S., *Juno and the Paycock: A tragedy in three acts* (Samuel French, London, 1932)

O'Rorke, K. P., 'Dublin Police', in *Dublin Historical Record*, vol. 29, no. 4, September 1976

Pigott, R., *Personal Recollections of an Irish National Journalist* (Hodges, Figgis, & Co., Dublin, 1882)

Reed, A., *The Irish Constable's Guide* (Alex Thom & Co., Dublin, 1895)

Report of the Dublin Disturbances Commission (London, 1914)

Report of the Trial of Robert Kelly for the Murder of Head Constable Talbot, at the City of Dublin Commission Court, October, 1871 (Dublin, 1873)

Robinson, H., *Memories: Wise and Otherwise* (Cassell, London, 1923)

Sinn Fein Rebellion Handbook (Weekly Irish Times, Dublin, 1916)

Stephens, J., *The Charwoman's Daughter* (Scepter Books, Dublin, 1912)

Sullivan, A. M., D. B. and T. D., *Speeches from the Dock, or Protests of Irish Patriotism*, Part 1 (Gill, Dublin, 1868)

Temple Thurston, E., *The Forest Fire and Other Stories* (Cassell, London and New York, 1919)

The Industries of Dublin, Historical, Statistical, Biographical. An Account of the Leading Business Men, Commercial Interests, Wealth and Growth (S. Blackett, London, 1887)

The Nature and Treatment of Rabies or Hydrophobia: Being the Report of the Special Commission appointed by the Medical Press and Circular with Valuable Additions (London, 1878)

Takagami, S., 'The Dublin Fenians: 1858–1879' (unpublished PhD thesis, Trinity College, Dublin, 1990)

Thorpe Porter, F., *Gleanings and Reminiscences* (Hodges, Foster, & Co., Dublin, 1875)

Tynan, P. J., *The Irish National Invincibles and their Times: Three Decades of Struggle Against the Foreign Conspirators in Dublin Castle* (Irish National Invincible Publishing Co., New York, 1894)

Watters, F., 'The Night of the Big Wind', *Journal of the Poyntzpass and District Local Society*, no. 7, May 1994, pp. 73–82

Welch, R., *The Abbey Theatre, 1899-1999: Form and Pressure* (Oxford University Press, Oxford, 1999)

White, J., *London in the Nineteenth Century: A Human Awful Wonder of God* (Random House, London, 2007)

Widdess, J. D. H., *The Richmond, Whitworth and Hardwicke Hospitals: St. Lawrence's Dublin, 1772–1972* (privately published, Dublin, 1972)

White, T. D. V., *The Road to Excess: A Biography of Isaac Butt* (Browne & Nolan, Dublin, 1946)

Wren, J., 'From Ballybough to Scurlogue's Bridge', *Dublin Historical Record*, vol. 37, no. 1, December 1983, pp. 14–29

Zimmermann, G. D., *Irish Political Street Ballads and Rebel Songs, 1780–1900* (Imprimerie La Sirène, Genève, 1966)

Newspapers, Almanacs and Journals

Belfast Newsletter

Bell's Life in Sydney and Sporting Chronicle

British Medical Journal, The

Cork Examiner, The

Dublin Almanac and General Register of Ireland for 1847

Dublin Evening Mail

Dublin Evening Packet

Dublin Magazine, The

Dublin Medical Press

Dublin Quarterly Journal of Medical Science

Dublin University Magazine, The

Evening Herald

Finn's Leinster Journal

Freeman's Journal, The

Illustrated Dublin Journal, The

Irish Fireside

Irish Independent

Irish Times, The

Kerry Evening Post

Leinster Express

Nation, The

Proceedings of the Pathological Society of Dublin

Saunders Newsletter

Sunday Independent

Times, The

Internet Sources

A Bill to Amend the Provision for the Government of Ireland, 27 July 1893, Section 29, http://www.dippam.ac.uk/eppi/documents/18823

http://www.dippam.ac.uk/eppi/documents/13652/download

Ireland–Australia Transportation Database, 'File of Thomas McNally (1837) and John Scott (1847)', www.nationalarchives.ie

Irish Statute Book, 'Dublin Police Act, 1836', www.irishstatutebook.ie/eli/1836/act/29/enacted/en/print.html

Royal Irish Constabulary, www.royalirishconstabulary.webs.com

Will Books, 1863 and 1864, http://www.willcalendars.nationalarchives.ie/search/cwa/index.jsp

INDEX

INDEX

INDEX

INDEX

INDEX

INDEX

ABOUT THE AUTHOR

Barry Kennerk graduated from Dublin City University with a PhD in history in 2014. His book *Moore Street: The Story of Dublin's Market District* (Mercier Press), published in 2012, garnered critical acclaim and was praised by the current Lord Mayor of Dublin, Nial Ring, as an authoritative work. Barry writes on an occasional freelance basis for newspapers at home and abroad including *The Irish Times* and *The New York Times*. He teaches English and history at Belvedere College, Dublin, and is married with two daughters.